MASTERPIECES
A Decade of Classics on British Television

MASTER

PIECES

*A
Decade
of
Classics on
British Television
By*

ALISTAIR COOKE

VNU BOOKS INTERNATIONAL | THE BODLEY HEAD | BH | LONDON | SYDNEY

Prepared and produced by VNU Books International, New York

Steven Murphy: *Executive Editor*

Jerry Mason: *Editor-in-Chief*
Albert Squillace: Art Director
Marion Geisinger: Picture Editor
Nancy Mack: Art Associate
Mary Carley: Editorial Associate

*The assistance of Sandra Ruch and the
Mobil Corporation is gratefully acknowledged.*

A VBI Book
Published by The Bodley Head, London, 1982

Thanks are due to the following for permission to reprint extracts from:
The Hedgehog and the Fox *by Isaiah Berlin, Weidenfeld & Nicolson Ltd.;
the Evelyn Waugh Beneficiaries for an extract from* Vile Bodies; *Cassell &
Co. for an extract from* Their Finest Hour *by Winston S. Churchill; Mills
& Boon Ltd. for an extract from* By A Gentleman with a Duster *by
Harold Begbie; the Proprietors of* Punch *for an extract from "The Havoc of
War", September 6, 1933.*

*British Library Cataloguing
in Publication Data*
Cooke, Alistair
Masterpieces
A Decade of Classics on British Television

1. Television programs–Great Britain–history and criticism. I. Title

791.45'0941   PN-1992.3.G7

ISBN 0-370-30476-4

Picture Credits

Cover: ©Bern Schwartz.

ATV Network: 95R, 96TL, 98L
Austrian Institute: 138.
Bibliothèque Nationale, Paris: 149.
Bibliothèque Spoel Berch de Lovenjoul, Chantilly, France: 102.
British Information Services: 218-219.
British Broadcasting Corp: 15, 16, 17B, 18L, 18R, 19L, 19R, 20, 24BL, 24BC, 24BR, 25BL, 25BC, 25BR, 26-27, 30, 36TR, 39, 44T, 44-45, 46-47, 47L, 49T, 50, 51, 52, 53, 54, 58, 59, 60BR, 64L, 64R, 65, 68L, 68TR, 69, 80-81, 81TL, 81TR, 83TR, 86-87, 87T, 87C, 87B, 88L, 88R, 91TR, 91BL, 91BR, 104L, 104R, 106, 107, 110, 111L, 113L, 115, 117L, 118L, 118C, 121L, 121R, 124, 126CR, 126BR, 129L, 129R, 130, 131R, 132, 133, 134, 135, 139, 140L, 140R, 151C, 151R, 157, 159TL, 159TR, 159B, 162L, 163, 164L, 164R, 166BL, 166BR, 171C, 171R, 174, 178TR, 178B, 179, 202, 205CL, 205CR, 205B, 206, 207, 208L, 208R, 210L, 212, 223TL, 223TR, 223CL, 223CR, 223B, 224
BBC Hulton Picture Library: 91TL, 99R, 145BR, 156R, 166T, 205T, 215TL.
Brown Brothers: 169.
Caisse Nationale Des Monuments Historiques et Des Sites, Paris: 113R.
Camera Press Ltd.: 221.
Courtauld Institute of Art, London: 48-49.
Culver Pictures: 196BR.
Dickens House, The, London: 70-71, 72TC, 72B.
From Sketch by John Doyle, 1847: 99L.
"The Queen of Cooks—and Some Kings" by Mary Lawton. Boni and Liveright, 1925: 171, 172, 176, 178TL.
"The Duchess of Jermyn Street" by Daphne Fielding, Little Brown and Company, 1964: 173.
Collection of Mrs. Michael Foot/J. R. Freeman: 167.
French Cultural Services: 109, 114, 117R, 118R, 120.
By Gracious Permission of Her Majesty the Queen, Copyright Reserved: 27, 47R, 49B.
Granada Television International: 215TR, 215B, 216, 217T, 217B.
Houghton Library, Harvard University: 60T, 60BL, 68BR, 80L.
Hughendon Manor, National Trust, England: 98R.
Imperial War Museum: 193TR, 193B.
International Instituut Voor Sociale Geschiedenis, Amsterdam: 162L.
Jane Austen's House/J. Butler-Kearney: 56R.
Kunsthistorisches Museum, Vienna: 12TL, 17T.
London Weekend Television: 142, 145T, 146TL, 146TR, 147, 148, 180, 186, 187T, 187B, 188, 189B, 190TL, 190TR, 190B, 191, 192B, 193TL, 194TL, 194TR, 194BL, 194BR, 195, 196TR, 196BL, 197T, 197BR, 198T, 198B, 199T, 199B, 219TL, 219BL, 219BR.
Mander & Mitchenson, London: 145BL.
MPG Collection: 24TL, 24TC, 24TR, 25TL, 25TC, 28, 33.
Museum of London, The: 12-13, 165.
National Gallery of Scotland: 38.
National Portrait Gallery: 25TR, 36TL, 95L.
New York Public Library: 12BL, 29T, 29B, 44B, 56L, 56-57, 63L, 63TR, 63BR, 72TL; Berg Collection, 81BL, 81BR, 83BL, 83BR, 84, 96TR, 96B, 146B, 192T; Print Division, 196TL.
Photoworld: 153, 189T.
Professional Picture Service: 111R, 123T, 123B, 126TL, 126TR, 131L, 151L, 197, 227, 228R.
Royal Hospital, Chelsea, London/A. C. Cooper: 43
Scala/Editorial Photocolor Archives: 23.
Tate Gallery, The: 210R.
Thames Television: 228L, 230, 231TR, 231B, 232, 234, 235.
Victoria and Albert Museum, Enthoven Collection: 72TR.
Viscount de L'Isle, from his collection at Penshurst Place, Kent, England: 36B.
Warburg Institute, The: 10.
By Courtesy of Mr. Simon Wingfield Digby, Sherborne Castle, Dorset, England: 34-35.
Worshipful Society of Apothecaries of London, The: 40-41.
Yorkshire Television Limited, © 1981: 70, 74T, 74B, 74, 75, 77T, 77B, 78T, 78B.

Contents

Part 4 The Edwardians

Part 5 Modern Times

Masterpiece Theatre Chronology

This is a book of critical essays about the authors (mainly) and the historical characters and events that have been dramatised on British television over the past ten years or more.

In Britain, the programmes were broadcast in no particular order, since—if for no other reason—they were the work of several producing companies: of the BBC mostly, but also of ATV, Granada, Thames, London Weekend, and Yorkshire Television. In the United States, they were all bought by the Public Broadcasting System (through a grant from the Mobil Corporation) and transmitted every Sunday evening at 9 p.m. local time over the entire network, which—with 292 stations—is now the largest television network in the country. The parent station for this enterprise was Boston's WGBH, and in the autumn of 1970 I was invited to be the m.c. or host for the programme, which was called Masterpiece Theatre. My function was to sketch in conversational language whatever literary, social, or plot background would be helpful in following the imminent episode. Since PBS allows no commercials, the commentaries required for plays that had been shown over the British commercial network were, ironically, longer than the ones for BBC productions.

The commentaries that accompany this family album of Masterpiece Theatre, though they pick up ideas and passages from my spoken introductions and extroductions, are written anew and are addressed to the wider—or narrower—audience that would like to recall the life and work of favorite authors and of authors forgotten or never attempted.

This brings up what is an undying argument about the sense or legitimacy of dramatising novels. Before television, it used to be an argument about adapting Shakespeare to the screen, the case for the prosecution being made in the most downright way by the English dramatic critic, the late James Agate: "If it is better for the masses to have bastard Shakespeare than no Shakespeare at all, then I must hold that 'I'm always chasing rainbows,' sung to the second subject of the *Fantaisie Impromptu,* is better than no Chopin . . . if it becomes lawful to lead the public to the Shakespearean well and see whether it will drink, I insist that the well be Shakespeare's and nobody else's. Let us not confuse this with the suggestion that bastard Shakespeare is Shakespeare. A sofa is not a bed because you can sleep on it. A film is not Shakespeare because it entertains the audience. . . . I refuse to believe that Hamlet's 'There are more things in heaven and earth, Horatio,' would be enhanced by sequences depicting Halley's comet and San Francisco's earthquake."

Like any good prosecutor, Agate is making an odious comparison between one thing done superbly and a different thing done fatuously. Even so, he has his points. There is no question that many movie and television producers tend (like television sponsors employing celebrity spokesmen) to hanker after distinguished originals in the hope that their distinction will brush off on the product. Both the movies and television are plagued by producers and directors whose talent lies in the precisely opposite direction from the one that is needed: they have an unerring gift for dramatising just those things that are least characteristic of the chosen author. And I myself share Agate's strong distaste for what has become a contemporary mania: the assumption that the forms of art are interchangeable, that a good short story will make a good ballet, a novel, a play, or worse—a complex political crisis, a rousing docu-drama.

But if television Tolstoy cannot possibly be the whole of Tolstoy, if we are always at the mercy of the director's taste as to what is quintessential and what is not, the new medium can, in discriminating hands, illumine nuances and intimacies in the relations between characters better, I should guess, than those that most people can pick up from the printed page. (Coppard and Bates are cases in point, much of Hardy, Flaubert, and Zola, certainly, and Henry James most of all—for a reason special to him that I have gone into in the later essay.) And, there is a beginning art of television acting, a small-scale refinement of movie acting, as different from stage acting as improvisation. The superlative television play has yet to be written and acted. But there have been some splendid beginnings. And it is not too fulsome to say that some of them have been seen on Masterpiece Theatre.

Also, as an unexpected by-product of the whole project, vast numbers of people who watched the plays, whether or not they approved of the adaptations, were moved to go to the originals. Robert Graves's *I, Claudius* was the most startling example. Contrary to the prejudice of book publishers, critics, and school teachers that television would drive out the habit of reading, and in the rising generation supplant it, television viewers made a beeline for the bookstores to obey the old injunction in reverse: "You saw the movie, now read the book." The fans of Masterpiece Theatre were conspicuous and willing victims of this reflex. So much so that booksellers were embarrassed by an incessant demand for authors long forgotten or out of print or known only to tiny publics. *Vanity Fair* was an early beneficiary of its exposure on television, and after the first showing of a Dorothy Sayers mystery the bookstores of America were ransacked for every adventure of Lord Peter Wimsey. By the time *I, Claudius* came along, the publishers had learned their lesson. Paperback reprints were stacked high against the anticipated invasion. Within a month of the showing of the early episodes, *I, Claudius* was at the top of the trade paperback fiction best-seller list, and a few weeks later its successor, *Claudius the God,* was a close second. I cannot believe that this has been a bad thing.

Apart from saying that these essays follow, more or less, the chronological order of their subjects, all that remains is a note of gratitude to various helpers on the television project and on the making of this book. I resist exposing many hard-working people to the embarrassment, and the reader to the tedium, of the Oscar winner who feels compelled to pay tribute to his highly paid colleagues, friends old and new, his studio boss, his wife and pre-school children, and his mother and father for having had him. But there are one or two people it would be churlish to overlook. Christopher Sarson, of WGBH, Boston, had a hard time persuading me to take on the job as host to the series. When I first turned it down and suggested that what he needed was somebody with the artful offhandedness of Max Beerbohm, or the zest of John Mason Brown, or the talkative guile of Alexander Woollcott, he stumped me with the clinching retort that they were all dead. After him, Joan Wilson became the producer and has remained so for eight of the ten years: an unfooled judge of television drama and a patient and tactful friend through good times and bad. Mobil's Herb Schmertz has been the best sort of patron: loyal and unobtrusive, never once questioning our choice of play or author. Steven Murphy had the idea for this book and its layout and was undeterred by what at times seemed final setbacks. Albert Squillace and Marion Geisinger, as will appear, have a genius for ferreting out prints and photographs that uncannily match the actors' impersonations. Finally, I must pay a special tribute to my editor, Charles Elliott, who, since the first page of my *America* was turned in, has been a scrupulous overseer and a wise and uncomplaining helper.   *A.C.*

Part 1

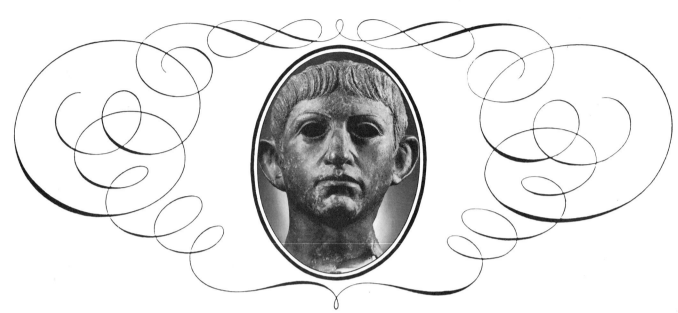

Emperors & Soldiers

I, Claudius

For most of the fifty-odd years during which he has been a voluntary exile at the foot of a mountain in Majorca, Spain, Robert Graves has looked like a prototypal sea captain, a weathered oak of a man with a leonine face, ropy hair, and the brusque hauteur of a man used to exercising command. The persona is not at odds with his character or his life work.

On the seas of Biblical and classical scholarship he has charted a daring, often a scandalous, course, as with his fictional life of Christ, *King Jesus*. He has teased and disdained the Establishment, whether as the keeper of the received knowledge about the Greek myths or as the dispenser of honorary degrees. As a literary historian, he has rewritten the *Iliad* in the form of a novel composed by a team of satirists, and has given Milton a wounding black eye through the pages of an imagined diary written by his wife. As a social historian taking two millennia for his gamut, he has re-created the first eighty years of the Roman Empire and written a heterodox account of Britain between the First and Second World Wars (*The Long Week-End*). Most of all, as a poet, he first propounded the theory that poetry is a therapy for problems unsolved in life, then rebelled against what he called the "Franco-American modernism" of Eliot and Pound and decamped to Spain to spend forty years strengthening and purifying the classical poetic forms. He has done this, moreover, with such passion and perfectionism (thirty-five drafts for every poem) that, after being relegated for decades to the status of a minor talent, he has emerged, in the judgment of more people than Stephen Spender, as one of the great English poets of the century and "the nearest thing we have to Latin poetry."

He was born in Wimbledon, in 1895, the third of five children of Amalie von Ranke (the grandniece of the German historian Leopold von Ranke) and Alfred Graves, a Scotch-Irish school inspector, a ballad writer, and the son of a Protestant bishop. He was sent to Charterhouse, one of the oldest of English public schools, where he was an energetic scholar and athlete and broke his nose in a boxing match. The First World War arrived when he was barely out of school. He was commissioned as a captain in the Royal Welch Fusiliers and after two grisly years in the trenches was sent home with a severe chest wound.

For twelve years thereafter he was an invalid, suffering from various respiratory ailments and a succession of nightmares that amounted to what he recalled as "an alternate life." In 1916 he put out the usual "slim volume" of a fledgling poet, followed it up with some sad and scathing war poems, and settled down—with a wife and four children—to a literary life near Oxford. He was there most of ten years until, increasingly pressed for money, he took his first

Portrait of Claudius in bronze. Although ungainly and burdened by physical afflictions, he was a learned man and proved a capable administrator when he became emperor, at 51, after the assassination of mad Caligula by the Praetorian Guard.

12

Symbols of Rome at the height of her power. Cameo
bears eagle emblem that also was carried throughout the empire
on the standards of the legion. Engraving shows the
Forum, the marble heart of Rome, in its glory. This was the center
from which the affairs of most of the known world were
ordered, where the gods were ritually propitiated,
and where men engaged in perilous struggles for power.
Aerial view, above, is a somewhat imaginary reconstruction of
Londinium, a military encampment and thriving small
town beside a river now called Thames. Claudius visited here
briefly in 43 A.D., giving imperial inspiration to the
campaign that made Britannia a province of Rome.

(and next to last) salaried job, as Professor of English Literature at the University of Cairo. He repented of this lapse into respectability within the year, returned to England, wrote a biography of T. E. Lawrence (of Arabia) and, in 1929, his tragi-ironic memoir of the war, *Goodbye to All That*. It was received as an act either of bravery or outrage, and it brought him fame and enough money to pay off his debts and move for keeps to Majorca and a permanent exile interrupted only during the Spanish Civil War and the Second World War by retreats into Switzerland, England, Brittany, and the United States. In Majorca, ever since, he has devoted himself to work of incomparable steadiness and versatility, plowing into the Greek and Hebrew myths, turning out novels and short stories and critical essays, a British soldier's view of the American Revolutionary War, a complete revision of the New Testament, and an immense historical grammar of woman as a poetical symbol in patriarchal and matriarchal societies (*The White Goddess*); and always, some part of every day, retreating with the ardor of a Franciscan monk to "the induced trance" of his poetry.

In the late 1950s, he went on several lecture tours of the United States and was delightedly received, at his own valuation, as a master craftsman of English poetry and prose, so that he was soon afterward rediscovered and reassessed in Britain by, as he put it, "repercussion from the United States." Sufficiently reinstated in the British pantheon, anyway, to be elected to the Poetry Chair at Oxford. We could say about him that he is "the last of the old-fashioned men of letters" if he has not already said it himself.

At this writing, he is a frail bulk of an Englishman in his late eighties, still living above the village of Deyá where he wrote *I, Claudius* in the early 1930s. There is a pretty conceit attached to its publication date.

In introducing the story, Graves imagined Claudius in old age, having written his memoir of the empire, going off to visit the Sibyl, the legendary prophetess, who tells him that his work will lie hidden "for nineteen hundred years or near" and then be revealed to an astonished world. When *I, Claudius* was published and some pedant quoted an encyclopedia to the effect that "the memoirs of Claudius, written in old age, have unfortunately been lost," Graves was able to say: "Quite the contrary. I dug them up and published them in 1934, 'nineteen hundred years or near,' just as the Sibyl prophesied."

Any narrative account of the Roman Empire, from its establishment by Augustus through the seventy-eight years (from 24 B.C. to 54 A.D.) that took in the subsequent reigns of Tiberius, Caligula, and Claudius, is bound to parade a cast of characters whose identities are as hard on the memory as their names

A wifely embrace by Livia (Sian Phillips) will bring no comfort to Caesar Augustus (Brian Blessed). She is plotting to make Tiberius, her son by an earlier marriage, the next emperor. "I, Claudius" was based on Robert Graves's imaginative history of Rome's first four emperors.

17

Praetorians hoist Claudius to their shoulders and
proclaim him emperor. Suetonius and Graves are agreed that
Claudius was terrified by this swift turn of fortune
but rose to the challenge. A first-century cameo (top) depicts
Claudius and wife Agrippina (Nero's mother) at left,
Tiberius and Livia (whose plot succeeded) at
right. Endangered species: Claudius (Derek Jacobi), Caligula
(John Hurt), and Emperor Tiberius (George Baker).

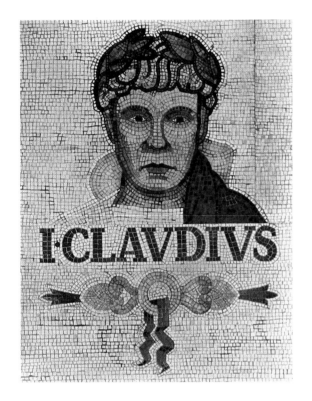

are hard on the ear. Moreover, the qualities that made Augustus the master of the known world are very difficult to dramatize, outside a four-night play cycle by Bernard Shaw. There was, in our dramatic version, only a hint here and there that Augustus was a military genius, a supreme architect of public works, a famous collector of fossils, an informed patron of the arts, a grateful intimate of Horace and Virgil, the creator of a constitution whose skeleton of self-government anticipated the framework of Western liberties, and an imaginative statesman who had Lincoln's gift for choosing the right generals at the right time, and Washington's gift for surrounding himself with the most adroit and wise politicians.

In this dramatic version, Augustus was seen as a burly, good-natured and baffled target for his wife's unyielding ambition to have her son Tiberius succeed to the throne; as a man barely able to turn around in a court of seething

This poster for program (left) took the form of a Roman mosaic. Claudius (right) and his wife, Messalina (Sheila White). She was the gift of Caligula and a notorious trollop. Claudius, the last to notice, finally acknowledged her debaucheries and had her executed.

intrigue before he must hatch or stifle another plot and bemoan another murder. This *I, Claudius* was frankly a story about the continuous collisions between the authority of the emperors and the private characters, ambitions, vices, and idiosyncrasies of their families, friends, and enemies. Jack Pulman, who wrote all the scripts, had the wit and the dialogue skill to stay close to the two endowments of Robert Graves that in the original novel guaranteed the ring of authenticity and the curiously engaging humanity of characters lost to us for centuries by their alien traditions and customs: namely, Graves's fidelity to his sources, Tacitus and Suetonius (of whom Graves is the classic English translator), and his brilliant virtuoso idea of having the imperial Romans talk in the familiar idiom of his own generation of British Empire builders.

There was one other obstacle to the showing of the series in the United States, which surprisingly crumbled overnight. By the time the series

*Scheming Livia, nearing her end, receives cold
comfort from her malevolent great-grandson, Caligula.
Right: Claudius close up. According to Graves, he survived
a half century of murder, treachery, and the whims of
madmen, and wrote "I, Claudius" as a memoir.*

appeared on the BBC, the British television public was inured to conventions of nudity and four-letter words that were by no means acceptable to Americans. Or, I'd better say, to their protectors, the American television network censors, who go under the wonderful euphemism of a department known as "Continuity Acceptance." In 1972, when *America,* my own television history of the United States, was shown simultaneously in both countries, several cuts had to be made for the American audience. No naked bathers could be shown performing the therapeutic rituals of a deadly solemn California commune. Not the most fleeting glimpse of naked breasts or buttocks on Las Vegas dancing girls. The branding of a yearling calf was thought offensive to the sensibilities of a large audience that, nevertheless, was very likely fond of veal.

So *I, Claudius* seemed to signal a thirteen-part onslaught on the decencies of American life. Sexual couplings were filmed in ceiling mirrors. An emperor's daughter was to be seen competing with a famous prostitute in the ritual exhaustion of the males of the imperial court. Orgies took place in full undress. Rape, incest, adultery raddled the plot of most episodes. Joan Wilson, the American producer of Masterpiece Theatre, and I cowered before the on-coming downpour of abuse. (The baring of one breast in *Jude the Obscure* had been "bleeped" in many cities of the United States, and, more recently, we had withstood the outrage of several viewers who saw, in the naive and rollicking *Poldark,* a sordid exercise in "bouncing from bed to bed.") The first episode of *I, Claudius* opened with a chorus of African dancing girls, naked from the waist up, helping Augustus celebrate the seventh anniversary of the Battle of Actium. We were warned by black friends that to begin our pudic breakthrough with semi-naked black girls would have gratuitously invited charges of, at best, racial condescension. It was cut. For the rest, I believe we cut only about two minutes of film in the whole thirteen hours. One entailed a gross bed scene, the other a vividly disgusting scene of Caligula disemboweling his pregnant sister and slavering with gobs of the murdered embryo—a lapse of taste un-common in BBC productions. Without this bit, the imagination could well supply what the visual image horribly rubbed in.

We awaited the storm. It was a very weak storm, and it came from the opposite direction. No outcry from the Moral Majority, but damnation wished on us as upstart dictators arbitrarily deciding who should see what. Who did we think we were, infringing the liberties of the subject? By 1977, it appeared, Justice Holmes's "moral climate of the time" had drastically changed. Happily, or lamentably, according to taste.

Death of an Emperor: His last wife, Agrippinilla (Barbara Young), and her infamous son Nero (Christopher Biggins) await Claudius's death. He was 64, and possibly sped on his way by poisoned mushrooms. Despite the era's bloody tumult, it would be 200 years before Rome declined and fell.

21

The Six Wives of Henry the Eighth

How a novel comes about has been exhaustively explained in a whole confessional literature by the practitioners themselves and/or by their biographers. A particular experience in one's own life is reshaped into a plot. A single friend, or a family, or a passing acquaintance suggests an ordeal of character or the weight of one character on a place, another life, a time. A persistent or transitory mood—of pleasure, tension, grief, penitence, guilt, whatever—in the life of the writer germinates a fantasy life. For a short-story writer, one incident or person observed is enough to suggest an episode complete in itself.

How a television drama comes about is, one might think, a more pedestrian routine. There is a staff of writers, or one writer, employed to cook up ideas and submit them to a producer, who calls in his staff, commissions the script, picks a director, chooses a cast.

The genesis of *The Six Wives of Henry the Eighth* is an early and interesting reflection of the freewheeling inventiveness of the BBC's drama department in what we can now see were its palmy days. Huw Wheldon, the managing director of BBC television in the late 1960s and early '70s, called the drama department "a hive of creativity," where programs were not spawned by "planning committees" but, most often, by the casual sparking of an idea by one person and the fanning of it by another "in the corridors, the offices, the clubs" of BBC's Television Centre. *Henry the Eighth,* for example, had first occurred to a staff producer who played with the notion of six episodes each devoted to a different wife. He was not sure it would have much popular appeal until he ran into a woman producer who remembered, from long ago, a quiz program on which various antiquarian experts were challenged to give an attribution to unidentified objects. One program was done in the Tower of London, and after it was over the contestants were relaxing in the central office when one of them noticed on the mantelpiece a silver codpiece. It had come loose from the chain mail of Henry the Eighth which, along with his armor, was prominently on display at the foot of a staircase. It had come loose because, in Wheldon's words, "generations of Cockney women had given it a bit of a rub on their way past. . . . If you're going to go past Henry the Eighth, you want to make a little bow toward fertility . . . for though, in point of fact, he never had very many children, he is thought of as a fertility symbol. He occupies a real position in the British consciousness." The memory of this was enough to impress the two producers and Wheldon that the thing could be done.

With these origins it was unlikely that the writers and directors would give us a play about those attributes that are independent of Henry's symbolic

*By confining his massive and splendidly arrayed
subject within an almost too-small frame, Hans Holbein
achieves a remarkable portrait of kingly power.
Henry was about 49, in the year of his divorce from Anne
of Cleves and marriage to Catherine Howard.*

 INO ·ÆTATIS·   · SVÆ · XLIX

Catherine of Aragon

Anne Boleyn

Jane Seymour

Annette Crosbie

Dorothy Tutin

Anne Stallybrass

Anne of Cleves

Catherine Howard

Catherine Parr

Elvi Hale

Angela Pleasence

Rosalie Crutchley

Henry (Keith Michell) with Catherine Parr (Rosalie Crutchley), sixth wife and comfort of his declining years. Inset: Hans Roest painting of younger Henry about to meet Francis I on sumptuous Field of the Cloth of Gold (1520).

reputation: a fine musician, a remarkable athlete, linguist, mathematician; a statesman of imagination and industry who unified the government of England, Wales, and the northern provinces and whose foresight in building a navy made possible the later defeat of the Spanish Armada and opened the Atlantic to the colonizing of America; a theological scholar subtle enough to find plausible pretexts, other than his ire at the Pope and his fear of Spain, for wanting to break with Rome. Such a study must be left to the books, pending the arrival of a spectacularly gifted playwright who can succeed—where most serious historical and political dramas fail—in breaking the usual stalemate between the complexity of historical truth and the emotional requirements of the stage and screen.

  If this series made colorful play with the romantic intrigues of the court, it did much to counter the stereotype of Henry as a Don Juan, a compulsive womanizer who deeply dislikes women and is plagued only by the itch to conquer

28

*Opposite: Catherine of Aragon defends herself
spiritedly at a church trial to establish grounds for divorce.
Above: Anne Boleyn shrinks from sentence of death.
Top: Cameo of fond father Henry with sickly Prince Edward,
the only male offspring of six marriages.*

Some four years after the Holbein portrait,
King Henry has aged perceptibly. While still a regal presence,
he suffers a variety of ailments and 20-year-old
Catherine Howard is as much nurse as wife. Servitor
Will Somers (Howard Goorney) attends his liege.

and move on. Henry was shown as a man genuinely fond of a variety of women, often as lover, sometimes as friend and companion: a man who did not want a mistress so much as a wife and a splendid male heir. He was greatly in love with his first wife, Catherine of Aragon, but she could give him only a daughter. Unfortunately, too, she was the aunt of Charles the Fifth of Spain, the chief Catholic king of Europe and head of the Holy Roman Empire. So when Henry wished to divorce Catherine, the Pope, fearing the power of Spain, jibbed at letting him have it. It was the status of Catherine as a Spanish princess that provoked Henry to defy the Pope, dissolve the English monasteries, confiscate all their wealth, set up his own independent Church of England, and procure a divorce through the offices of the new homegrown Pope, so to speak, he had now at his elbow, namely the Archbishop of Canterbury.

Thereafter, we saw him restlessly seeking a son and failing with Anne Boleyn, who also produced a daughter (the future Elizabeth the First, no less) and was beheaded on a very dubious charge of adultery. After her, Jane Seymour, a saintly young woman who, as a contemporary wrote, "was obnoxious to no one, gave birth to a puny child, the future Edward the Sixth, and then died." Henry's next choice was narrowed by the fact that France was always losing to Spain, and Spain was the master of Europe—and the Pope. Accordingly, Henry sent Hans Holbein the Younger off to draw the likeness of two daughters of a German duke. He married one of them, Anne of Cleves, but when it became clear that France and Spain had abandoned any plan to invade England, he divorced her.

It is a moot point whether his last two wives were sterile or whether the aging Henry had already succumbed to the sickness that afflicts aging men: the urge to prove the virility they no longer have. At any rate, no sons appeared. His fifth choice was Catherine Howard, the niece of his chief adviser, the Duke of Norfolk. (An incidental irony of this alliance is the fact that to this day Norfolk is the first peer of England, the Earl Marshal who presides over coronations, royal marriages and funerals—and his is still the leading Catholic family of the United Kingdom.) Henry ended the chase by seeking a wife who should be above all a nurse and companion and found her in Catherine Parr, a twice-married lady, a divinity student, and a devotee of the New Learning. We saw the once lusty monarch feeble and ulcerated. This visible emphasis on old age was not, however, that of the scriptwriter but of the sixteenth century, when the expectation of life at birth was about thirty-five years. It may console some men, and terrify others, that when Henry the Eighth died he had reached the enormous age of fifty-six.

31

Elizabeth R

This series immediately followed the Tudor cycle that ended, in our dramatization, with the death of Henry the Eighth.

If Henry is a role that few bulky actors can resist, that of Queen Elizabeth the First has hypnotized generations of actresses of several countries and dramatists and operatic composers from Rossini to Maxwell Anderson. In the movies alone, she has been played by Sarah Bernhardt, Flora Robson, Florence Eldridge, Bette Davis, Agnes Moorehead, Irene Worth, and Jean Simmons. If none of them has been specially memorable, it must be because the historical character calls for a range of traits seldom found in one woman and never in a single actress: intellectual power, secretiveness, generosity, stinginess, a peasant shrewdness, courage, deviousness, tenderness, inflexibility, authority softened by irony, vanity tempered by self-knowledge. In this television series, it is fair to say, Glenda Jackson, playing with spunkiness, intelligence, and an engaging guile, had nothing to fear from her predecessors.

That Elizabeth ever got to the throne must have seemed as unlikely in her youth as that Captain Mark Phillips will be the next King of England. The line of succession, laid down in Henry's will, did not offer much natural hope to Elizabeth. It was to go from his children, Edward and Mary, through their issue. Edward, always sickly, died at fifteen, plainly without issue, but not before he had amended the succession to bar his sisters forever and to elevate Lady Jane Grey "and her heirs male" to the true line. When this plan was overthrown, Mary succeeded and for several years the prospect of a male heir must have appeared certain. From girlhood on, Mary had been engaged in turn to Francis the First of France then to Charles the Fifth of Spain, then to Francis's son. Finally, after years of isolation bereft of fiancés, and after the death of her brother, she married Philip, the son of Charles the Fifth of Spain and, as Queen, set about restoring the Church of Rome. Several times during her reign, the court was agog with the certain news of her pregnancy, but she was evidently a distinguished case of pseudo cyesis. There were no heirs, male or female.

All this while, Elizabeth had been subjected to a series of ordeals that would have driven a more delicate child insane. Her mother was beheaded, and she herself declared a bastard. She was twice "examined" for evidence of treason. She was imprisoned in the Tower of London to await execution, and afterward put under house arrest. She was often the intended victim of forced marriages and of assassination plots. What put her at last on the throne was nothing more or less than Mary's obsessive drive to abolish the Church of England and restore

*Queen Elizabeth had her father's fair skin and golden
hair and his capacity for working and playing hard. She spoke
four languages, enjoyed the chase, could not
be wearied at the dance, and ruled efficaciously in
the sunlit years of England's Renaissance.*

England to Rome. During the last three years of Mary's life, the persecution of influential Protestants was unremitting, and when she died the blood of over three hundred martyrs was on her hands.

So, we are told, "on Mary's death, Elizabeth's accession was welcomed with almost universal rejoicing." "Universal" is going a little far. But in England Elizabeth was welcomed not so much as a character (about which little was known) but as a blessed relief from a quarter century of rebellion, murderous pretenders, royal executions, the fear of the Pope, and the fear that the throne would pass to France or Spain, one or other of the two great powers of Europe. It took a long time for the last two fears to abate. Even after Mary's persecutions, England was split between the old loyalists to Rome and the new converts to the Church of England. The dead queen's widower, King Philip of Spain, went on the assumption that Henry the Eighth's Church of England was a whimsical interruption in England's allegiance to Rome, and he began at once to choose a suitable Catholic suitor for Elizabeth.

This assumption was an actual threat to the sovereignty of England. It was based on the fact—which the glitter of Elizabeth's coronation masked for the moment—that England was at the lowest ebb of its power. The religious upheaval and the steady defeats in the war with France had saddled the country with an enormous government debt. England had become a maverick Protestant island, and the most loyal of Elizabeth's advisers were hagridden by the fear that unless she married some dependable big ally, preferably a Catholic, England would eventually be invaded and conquered by either France or Spain. But a husband from either nation could have easily asserted his status as a gauleiter of his native land and a legate of Rome. Marriage could have turned her from a queen into a consort, and it is probably the reason why Elizabeth chose to remain—and according to all the best evidence did truly remain—a Virgin Queen.

She was the first English monarch to have the sense, the strategical sense, to maintain the Protestant faith and yet treat her Catholic citizens as good and loyal Englishmen. This tolerance extended remarkably to Mary Stuart, daughter of the King of Scotland, queen consort of France, proclaimed in Paris "the Queen of England," who was allowed to live in England as half-guest, half-prisoner and foment innumerable plots against the Queen and English independence. It is a marvel that Elizabeth resisted for nineteen years chopping off her cousin's head. But after this final insult to the most powerful Catholic pretender, the aging Philip of Spain decided once for all to put an end to Elizabeth's intransigence by invading England. He had conquered Portugal and thus ac-

Preceding pages: Ruffed, brocaded, and pearled,
Elizabeth is borne on the shoulders of court gentlemen.
Opposite: Dancing lady is the Queen, with her Robin—Robert
Dudley (played by Robert Hardy, top right).
Portrait (top) is a later favorite, the Earl of Essex.

37

38

quired an oceangoing fleet with the best seamen in Europe. With them, he was convinced, he could annihilate the modest English navy. What he had not taken into account was the cunning and persistence, over many years, of Elizabeth's diplomacy: her wooing of French kings, her bolstering the power of the Dutch against Spain, the exercises in initiative she had given to that modest navy by secretly encouraging such pirates as Drake and Hawkins to raid the Spanish on the high seas. All this had sapped the power of Spain to mount a successful invasion. Its failure marks a shift in the balance of power as historic as that of Waterloo or the Communist takeover of China. With the defeat of the Armada, the legendary Elizabethan Age began and our continuous dramatic story ended.

      The last episode, finding Elizabeth in old age, is of the sort that few actresses can bear to forgo, but Glenda Jackson resisted the usual croaking and paltering behind a chalk-white mask. What her performance did offer, however, were some reflections on the comparative horrors of old age in the early seventeenth century, and the desperate devices whereby elegant ladies sought to disguise them. We had watched Elizabeth go from a spirited seventeen-year-old to a very aged woman in her seventieth year. Seventy in those days was a hundred in ours. Medicine was a matter of leeches and purgatives.

Above: Mary Stuart, Queen of Scots, dies under the headsman's ax at Fotheringhay Castle. Complex, fascinating, ill-fated, she was nonetheless a relentless plotter against Elizabeth's throne. Right: Gloriana (Glenda Jackson) hides her decrepitude under a cosmetic mask.

Dentistry did not exist. Everybody had brown teeth. Elizabeth's were evidently worse than most. Elizabeth was seen at the end in a clownlike mask. But it was a nonremovable mask. Bathing was not a fashion of the time, and when she died it was precisely calculated that Elizabeth had more than half an inch of permanent makeup on her face. Her formula has come down to us: "a lotion made of white of egg, powdered eggshell, alum, borax, and poppy seeds mixed with mill water."

She was never a beauty. She often said so, but like women both domestic and liberated, she never disputed compliments to her beauty. She piled hundreds of jewels on her person, one thing in which any dramatization provides only a pale reflection of the reality. Francis Bacon, not a noticeably cruel man,

Defense of the realm: As Elizabeth and her land
army await the outcome (left), England's faster ships, greater
firepower, and superior tactics assure Spain's historic
defeat. The armada was en route to Holland to provide cross-Channel
transport for the Duke of Parma's invasion force.

wrote: "She imagined that the people, who are much influenced by externals, would be diverted by the glitter of her jewels from noticing the decay of her personal attractions."

It is probably impossible, even at this late date, to exaggerate the genius of Elizabeth as a geo-political statesman. She inherited a bankrupt island kingdom of about the standing, even as a European power, of Holland or Sweden today. She left it as one of the ranking powers of Europe, and the impulse given to overseas colonizing by the new strength of her navy generated an urge to roam, to conquer, to govern, which made Britain within three centuries the most powerful nation on earth, in possession of a vast empire that was liquidated only by the Second World War.

This was the series that, early in 1971, gave birth to Masterpiece Theatre. Looking back on it now, I sometimes marvel that it did not strangle the program in its cradle. The script was not a masterpiece, either original or adapted. The story, of religious, political, and military turbulence in late-seventeenth- and early-eighteenth-century England, was one of tortuous complexity that often defied dramatization. Apart from Susan Hampshire, who brought alternately strong and wistful echoes of *The Forsyte Saga,* there was hardly a recognizable actor or actress. The swift and constant switches of the plot among England, France, and Holland were not helped by the now universal convention of what is called the "jump cut," whereby D. W. Griffith's brilliant inventions of the fade-out (end of day or end of scene) and the dissolve (transition to another place or time) are scorned in favor of an instantaneous jump from one frame to the next, whether the second shot is of another actor in the same room or a new scene in another country. And if the jump cut was, in this filming, the enemy of lucidity in telling a story, the general confusion was compounded by a curious decision of the producers to put most of the men in black wigs and sometimes have them pronounce their best lines with their backs to the audience. Add to this that almost all the men spoke in either a harsh or mellifluous Southern British English of our own day. There were times when it required almost a sixth sense to know if we were listening to the Dutch King of England (who, in life and in England, spoke only French) or Louis the Fourteenth, or our hero, John Churchill himself.

Yet the play moved at a confident pace, the characters—once they could be recognized—were sharply drawn. The production was gaudy with splendid sets and pretty women. There was, throughout, the sense that something both serious and entertaining was going on.

This was due, I believe, to the author's skill in tying the continuing theme (the struggle to suppress all Catholic uprisings and secure a Protestant throne) to several characteristics of the story and the period that would have a special appeal to a general audience.

One was the practice, bizarre to us but necessary to a nation desperate to secure the Protestant succession, of shopping all over Europe for its kings and queens. Indeed, the need to intermarry with other royal houses produced a continuum in which the rulers of most of the warring nations of Europe, so late as the twentieth century, were either uncles or nephews or cousins of each other. The present Queen Elizabeth has generations of German blood in her veins, and when her father—George the Sixth—married a Scottish noblewoman (the Queen

John Churchill, Duke of Marlborough, a superb strategist, led the alliance which checked the military power of Louis XIV on the Continent. John Closterman's painting shows the duke's prancing horse treading the French flag while airborne beings celebrate overhead.

44

John and Sarah Churchill: John Neville and Susan
Hampshire played the duke and his lady, the tempestuous
"torpedo in skirts." Opposite: An engraving of
Charles II and his intimates is approximated
by the cast. The dog is a King Charles spaniel.

Mother is a direct descendant of Robert the Bruce) there was great rejoicing in Britain that at last an English prince had not gone to Europe in search of a wife.

There were also some telling analogies, particularly pointed to Americans, between the politics of seventeenth-century England and twentieth-century America. For example, the discovery that Charles the Second, usually thought of as a nearly absolute monarch, had much the same relation with Parliament as that of the President of the United States with the House of Representatives: he had the grandeur, but Parliament held the purse strings. He might storm and speechify, but on any money bill he was ultimately at the mercy of the Lord Treasurer, the counterpart of the chairman of the House Ways and Means Committee.

In the popular reception of William of Orange as King of England, and the subsequent disillusionment in a man who said, "I don't like the English and they don't like me," Americans did not have to strain to recognize their own experience of regularly electing a savior who, within a year or two, turns out not to be the new Moses.

*Opposite: Charles II (James Villiers) was the first
of four monarchs of Britain for whom Churchill performed
soldierly services. Above: Ermine-clad King
holds audience. Painting shows Charles's brother as the Duke of
York, before he became the stubborn, unpopular James II.*

*Triptych shows three stages of the Battle of Blenheim,
Marlborough's supreme triumph. The baton-waving duke is on rearing
horse in right-hand panel. Opposite: Churchill at Blenheim,
and miniature of Queen Anne and her consort. While victory
elated England, Anne was under pressure to halt the war.*

In Titus Oates, an archetype of what in our time has come to be known to lawyers as a litigious paranoiac, it was not fanciful to see a monster seventeenth-century Joseph McCarthy. Oates was a small Anglican clergyman who went abroad for a while and posed as a Catholic long enough to piece together many influential names and invent a conspiracy. He then went into the wholesale business of forging letters and documents. He was called before the Privy Council and expounded on forty-three separate plots. There was usually just enough truth to make some of his cases plausible and a few perilous. The rumors took beyond his best hopes, and he boosted the number of conspiracies to eighty-two. Finding himself, in high circles, hailed as a great patriot and, among the people, as the savior of the nation, he dared to accuse the Queen of high treason. His fabricating talent overreached itself, but not before thirty or forty more or less innocent people had been put to death. He lost large damage suits. The witch hunt spent itself. He was committed to prison, then released, censured by the House of Lords, denied his pension, expelled from even the Baptist church, and died unsung and unnoticed.

51

Through all this, the rather idealized figure of John Churchill passed first as a handsome soldier hiring himself out to any monarch with the money to pay; then as a devoted husband to a lady-in-waiting at court; climactically as the hero of the Battle of Blenheim, which broke the French power in Europe as certainly as Elizabeth had broken the Spanish; in the end, as the failed Whig enemy of the Tories, a discredited great name pottering about the immense, unfinished palace of Blenheim, on which a grateful nation had lavished a fortune, and on which his wife—"a torpedo in petticoats"—was to spend twenty-four years in the teeth of striking workmen, huge debts, and the ridicule of her contemporaries.

It would be coy to ignore the main attraction of the title of this series. Always, in the movement of John Churchill, we saw foreshadowed the lumbering figure of his most famous descendant. And the first breathtaking shot of Blenheim was a warm reminder of that evening in 1875 when a beautiful lady from Brooklyn, attending a ball against her doctor's orders, retired in a hurry to the chaplain's bedroom and gave birth to Winston Spencer Churchill.

*"Mrs. Freeman" and "Mrs. Morley": Sarah was on
intimate and influential terms with Queen Anne (Margaret Tyzack),
while Churchill (opposite) upheld Britain's power abroad. Sarah
could not curb her tongue or her temper, and lost the Queen's regard
even as the duke fell a victim of Tory politics.*

Poldark

V ulnerable" is so much the favorite vogue word among movie and theatre critics that it may have been supplanted by the time this book is published. In one recent biographical dictionary of the cinema, it is applied no less than forty times, to vulnerables as far apart as Buster Keaton and Jeanne Moreau. It says something about our time (it says, perhaps, that all our heroes are antiheroes) that it is invariably used as a compliment, a modish substitute for what an earlier generation of critics called "sensitive."

It must, then, have come as a jolt to the more earnest fans of Masterpiece Theatre that—after a succession of vulnerable heroes and heroines in James, Hardy, Dostoyevsky, Tolstoy, Bates, and the rest—Captain Ross Poldark should have been embraced by millions as the resounding favorite of all our plays.

Poldark is a saga of gallantry and chicanery in late-eighteenth- and early-nineteenth-century Cornwall, then the copper-producing center of England.

Ross Poldark (Robin Ellis) and his Demelza (Angharad Rees) endured twenty-nine episodes of strenuous adventure before the villainous Warleggans got their just deserts and series came to happy end. Opposite: Poldark runs afoul of the French and is imprisoned as a spy.

Poldark comes home from service against the Americans in the Revolutionary War to find his father dead, his farmland run down, and—on the presumption that he himself had been killed—his mines about to be sold to a scheming family of stay-at-homes, the Warleggans. The whole story is about Poldark's uphill bravery in trying to pay off his father's debts, to care for his tenants, to rehabilitate the mines, to do his duty in the French wars, to break the "rotten borough" system of Parliamentary elections, and to resolve a private conflict between his feeling for an old flame of his own class and his love for an illiterate urchin he has taken in and succored.

Poldark is the creation of Winston Graham, a Lancashire boy who moved to Cornwall and now nourishes a passion for privacy in a large Victorian house and six acres of gardens in Sussex. He has made a living as a novelist since he was seventeen, has written half-a-dozen thrillers that were made into movies, and after the Second World War published the first of what developed as four volumes on the life and times of Ross Poldark. This splendid Scott–Henty–R. L. Stevenson saga has sold a million or more copies and is a favorite of the Finns and Japanese as well as of the British.

The appeal of *Poldark* can be plausibly explained, especially in hindsight. After a glut of guilt-ridden adulterers, corrupt aristocrats, temporizing politicians, dispossessed farmers, doomed students, and the like, Poldark appeared like a meteor on a murky night. He is a soldier whose manly instincts are only fleetingly clouded by misgivings or second thoughts. He is decent, plucky, generous, brisk, and positive. He sees in Warleggan a villain as straightforward as the Soviet Union. Whatever else he is, Poldark is not vulnerable. He is Ronald Reagan. In an unsettled and brooding time, his landslide election by a huge and grateful audience as favorite Masterpiece Theatre hero should not, after all, have been such a surprise.

53

Part 2

Nineteenth-Century Giants: England

Jane Austen
Pride and Prejudice

Jane Austen is by now so "safe" a classic that her dramatizers run the danger, as with Dickens, of assuming that the genius of the original is bound to show through any patchwork of parts. She, however, presents the film adapter and the art director with particular hazards. The art director, recalling the grace of Georgian domestic architecture and the froufrou elegance of Regency court costumes, is tempted to dress up Mr. Bennet like a prince consort and house his family in a country mansion well beyond the reach of a genteel upper-middle-class family of modest means. It was a temptation not always resisted in this glistening BBC version, so squeaky clean as to suggest at times a doll's house with doll-like emotions. This prettifying confronted the scriptwriter with the extra challenge of giving the story and its characters a verisimilitude beyond their skin-deep elegance.

Luckily, the challenge was met with almost disdainful ease. For *Pride and Prejudice* was dramatized, over four careful years, by Fay Weldon, a considerable novelist in her own right. She had come to Jane Austen fairly late and was well aware that she is one novelist who can be read too soon. In a note about the work, Miss Weldon explained why Jane Austen appears to many young readers remote and bewildering:

55

Partly because of the way in which it is written, partly because of the subtlety with which she examines the intricacies of human behavior, and mainly because the society she describes has gone forever. She anatomizes a world where women of a certain class can survive only through men—brothers, fathers, uncles, husbands—and are dependent upon marriage. Their only alternative is the ignominy of spinsterhood or of becoming a governess.

The chief technical problem for the adapter is that of dealing with a medium that is mainly one of dialogue. In all her novels, Jane Austen's narrator is a dual character: the heroine as participant and the heroine (J. A.?) as onlooker. What is fatal to all stage versions of Jane Austen is their dependence on dialogue: the participant cannot be seen also at the remove of the ironical commentator. Miss Weldon solved this by adopting the convention of having Elizabeth Bennet seen as the central character and heard as the "voice-over" commentator.

Best of all, Fay Weldon never leaves us in any doubt that she is adapting not a romantic novel but a parody of one. "Pictures of perfection," Jane once confided in a letter, "make me sick and wicked." This adaptation demonstrated a fine ear for the spare, exquisite language of the original and a ready talent for taking Jane's maliciously cheerful view of social pretension. The result was as true a rendering of the essential Austen as we are likely to get. Viewers who disliked this *Pride and Prejudice* do not like Jane Austen.

Elizabeth Bennet (Elizabeth Garvie) the heroine of
Jane Austen's second novel, "Pride and Prejudice,"
visits Netherfield, the country home of Mr. Bingley, to
take care of her ailing sister Jane. There she
again encounters Mr. Darcy and is piqued by the icy
hauteur he reveals to society.

She was born in a country parsonage in 1775, the seventh child of a clergyman who had scholarly connections with Oxford. Two of her brothers were sailors, frequently involved in naval battles with the French, and both of them became admirals. But they were the only ones of the family who came close to being public figures. It was a very private family and a secluded one, never aiming at high society or a public life. True, Jane regularly "visited"—lived for several years in Bath, which Beau Nash had made a fashionable resort. And she lived for a while in London. Too much can be made of Jane as an Emily Dickinson recluse. She was contented with her spinster's domestic life. She not only traveled very little, and never very far, but she chose to forswear her own knowledge of London, Bath, Southampton, and other such fashionable places for a country cousin's wide-eyed view of them. This was a deliberate device. For the satirical requirements of the writing she made her own: "Three or four families in a country village," she wrote, "are the very thing to work on." As far as she was concerned, they represented a microcosm of the human family.

She began to write in her early teens—mostly short burlesques of what she admired, and what she didn't, in her reading. She had read widely in her father's library. The Greek and Latin classics. Some Italian. French she read

Elizabeth's profession of love for Darcy surprises
Mr. Bennet, in this 1833 illustration for "Pride and Prejudice."
An engraved portrait of Jane Austen, looking like one of her
characters. Right: A contemporary painting of Austen family's
home, Chawton Manor, in the Hampshire countryside.

easily. And, as a late-eighteenth-century girl, she was familiar with Fielding, Smollett, Sterne, Richardson, all the early and bawdy novelists that clergymen of the next generation but one, the Victorians, would keep locked up if they had not already made a bonfire of them the day their first daughter was born. Jane was an expert needlewoman; she played the piano, went to dances, flirted some of the time; but all the time she quite simply and systematically watched the fusses and follies of the people around her and invented in that rectory an intimate form of satirical novel.

Her early stories, including the first draft of at least three of her famous novels, were written expressly for the amusement of her family. Reading aloud was the prime form of home entertainment and, in Jane's case, was a larky communal substitute for the private pleasure we all take in gleaning the foibles of our friends from their letters. Her busiest time was between the ages of nineteen and twenty-four, when she wrote the first versions of *Sense and Sensibility, Pride and Prejudice,* and *Northanger Abbey.* For twelve years thereafter none of them was published, and some viewers of *Pride and Prejudice* were quick to wonder whether, as a woman, she had an uphill battle getting published at all.

58

Well, there is no sense from her letters that she felt herself to be a freak as a female novelist or a martyr as an unpublished one. She thought of herself as an amateur writing on peculiar and private themes, certainly not the sort of thing that would fetch the novel-reading public, which in Jane's day expected and got—from the two big professional best-sellers, Maria Edgeworth and Ann Radcliffe—overwrought Gothic romances complete with abandoned waifs and strangers of mysterious origins. Jane, indeed, mocked these conventions by introducing one of her heroines as almost underprivileged, since "there was not one family among [her] acquaintance who had reared and supported a boy accidently found at their door—not one young man whose origin was unknown."

It is true that two publishers sat on her novels for four or five years.

Above: The pride of Mr. Fitzwilliam Darcy (David Rintoul) has moderated; the prejudice of Miss Elizabeth Bennet (Elizabeth Garvie) has been overcome. Opposite: Elizabeth's winsome smile reveals her pleasant wit, but belies her fears about the course of true love.

PRIDE

AND

PREJUDICE:

A NOVEL.

IN THREE VOLUMES.

BY THE

AUTHOR OF "SENSE AND SENSIBILITY."

VOL. I.

London:

PRINTED FOR T. EGERTON,
MILITARY LIBRARY, WHITEHALL.
1813.

*Top: A drawing of giddy Mrs. Bennet and two of her five
unmarried daughters, from 1894 edition. Daughters Lydia, Jane,
and Mary were played by Natalie Ogle, Sabina Franklyn,
and Tessa Peake-Jones. Left: Anonymous title
page of first edition, published, belatedly, in 1813.*

But it's also true that she put out her books without her name on the title page, not because she was a woman but because she wanted to be anonymous. When at last *Sense and Sensibility* came out, in her thirty-sixth year, it had on the title page: "A Novel by a Lady." Then *Pride and Prejudice* "By the Author of *Sense and Sensibility*," then *Mansfield Park* "By the Author of *Sense and Sensibility* and *Pride and Prejudice*." And so on.

All her novels except *Northanger Abbey* and *Persuasion* were published in the last six years of her life; the last two after her death, at the age of forty-one. So, even if they had been literary sensations, the knowledge of her own fame would have been brief. In fact, she was barely known to the reading public. After her death her works were enjoyed by a tiny cult; rather like, I should guess, the audience today, or yesterday, for the novels of L. H. Myers. This cult did, however, a score or so years after she died, include some giants. Macaulay was one. Sir Walter Scott was another. He wrote in his journal in 1837:

Read again, and for the third time at least, Miss Austen's finely written novel of *Pride and Prejudice*. . . . The big Bow-Wow strain I can do myself like any now going; but the exquisite touch, which renders ordinary things and characters interesting . . . is denied me.

In that year, Queen Victoria came to the throne, and the Victorians, finding Jane's language outdated and her themes old-fashioned, didn't take to her. In retrospect, we can see why they mightn't. Popular education, the rise of a merchant class, the first spate of journalism, made the eighteenth-century mandarin style seem antiquated, with its upper-crust irony and cadenced sentences. Jane was an eighteenth-century woman who satirized the fulsome feelings the Victorians came to wallow in. Dickens, the author-hero of his time, ends most of his romances on a lovey-dovey note that Jane would have giggled at. As witness the tart last sentences of *Pride and Prejudice* ("a lighthearted book, written in 1796, when I was twenty-one"):

Happy for all her maternal feelings was the day on which Mrs. Bennet got rid of her two most deserving daughters. . . . I wish I could say, for the sake of her family, that the establishment of so many of her children produced so happy an effect as to make her a sensible, amiable, well-informed woman for the rest of her life; though perhaps it was lucky for her husband, who might not have relished domestic felicity in so unusual a form, that she still was occasionally nervous and invariably silly.

This was not at all suited to the taste of the long Victorian age. Jane's small circulation dwindled and vanished. Not until the first decade of this century, mainly at the prompting of the Shakespearean scholar A. C. Bradley, was she suddenly and widely rediscovered, and rejoiced in.

61

William Makepeace Thackeray
Vanity Fair

"A Novel Without a Hero" was the subtitle that Thackeray gave to *Vanity Fair* when it came out as a single book after its appearance in monthly parts between 1847 and 1848. It is also the daring innovation, in Victorian England, of a novel without a heroine, for Amelia Sedley, the rich girl, is passive and vacillating, and Becky Sharp is poor but pretentious, genteel but on the make, one of the most accomplished bitches in fact or fiction between the fall of Rome and the rise of Las Vegas. What sort of man could have created this engaging monster? If it were possible for a shrewd reader to come on *Vanity Fair* without any knowledge of its author, he might make an educated guess that he was reading a strangely elegant translation from Balzac. But if you had met the author in one of his clubs, you might have taken him to be a kindly middle-aged clergyman on his vacation.

William Makepeace Thackeray was then thirty-six, with a pink moon of a face and twinkling glasses: a plump gentleman tabby cat of impeccable pedigree. Breeding exhaled from him like a very faint but all the more delicate perfume. (In one of his very rare moments of malice he said something that rankled in its victim for years: he remarked that in a marvelously rich and varied gallery of characters, "Mr. Dickens has never pictured a gentleman.")

He was born in Calcutta, in 1811, the son of an administrator in the East India Company, who died four years later. While his mother stayed behind in India, mainly to catch in marriage an engineer she had mooned over for years, the boy was sent home to relatives in London and drifted unhappily from one private school to another. However, the makings of a melancholic were dispersed for the time being in a happy two years at Cambridge, after which he made an improving tour of France and Germany and returned to the Middle Temple to study law. He was not much given to the law, nor to any other profession, so long as he was well provided for and could amble along in the sure expectation that, on his twenty-first birthday, he would receive—as he did—an inheritance of twenty thousand pounds from his father. He fiddled with essay writing, he dabbled more promisingly in painting and drawing, but once he had his money he settled to two hobbies: gambling and daring speculations in the India agencies. Within two years, the failure of his bank in Calcutta compounded his gambling losses and, at the age of twenty-three, he had nothing of his own and nothing coming in.

To someone like Thackeray, nourished always on, at the least, a handsome supply of what is now called "walking money," the lack of it from any source was a social disaster. He was the armchair crony of scholars, peers, soldiers,

The plump, benign Thackeray of this water-color portrait
would seem to be unacquainted with the raffish world of
"Vanity Fair." Frederick Barnard's painting
shows a genteel Becky with sheathed claws. Title page of
"A Novel Without a Hero" is from the 1849 first edition.

lawyers, and other nicely fixed and refined young men. The suddenly impoverished son of the gentry is not an unfamiliar type even today, but in Thackeray's day and to members of his caste, money was either there or it was to be acquired in a very few socially acceptable ways. He had only one choice, and it was an appalling one—he would have to earn a living. To us, looking back across the wide plain of the welfare state, where everybody has more or less what he needs, to the heights of early-nineteenth-century English society, where there were top people sunning on the mountains and bottom people sweating in the valleys, such a fate does not wring our hearts. Yet Thackeray accepted it without self-pity, alone in Paris living in a dingy room and beginning to draw very well. There he met a poor Irish girl and married her. His stepfather came to his rescue by buying a newspaper so that Thackeray could stay on in Paris as its correspondent. The paper failed.

Becky (Susan Hampshire) fails in quest for money
from her husband's wealthy aunt, Miss Crawley (Barbara Couper,
right), but succeeds with degenerate Lord Steyne (Robert
Flemyng, left). Opposite: Adoring Amelia (Marilyn Taylerson)
and her conceited husband George (Roy Marsden).

He came back to London with his wife, and, seeing all the new magazines mushrooming for the amusement of the new audience of a growing middle class, he decided to become a journalist. Either that, or an illustrator, or both. On a day in 1837, he took a sheaf of drawings and called on a young man who, if he was not yet a literary lion, was a very sprightly young lion cub, known as Boz. Charles Dickens was then twenty-five and had been hired to write the text to accompany some sporting plates to be done by the famous Seymour. After the first monthly issue of this oddity, called *The Posthumous Papers of the Pickwick Club,* the author was more famous than the artist. Seymour committed suicide, and Dickens looked around for a new illustrator. Years later, Thackeray recalled "walking up to his chambers in Furnival's inn with two or three drawings in my hand, which, strange to say, he did not find suitable."

During the next three years, Thackeray established himself, as a journalist, with a steady flow of essays, burlesques, fictional memoirs (of a Cockney footman, of a British soldier in India), and romantic crime stories. He would not again go hungry, but whatever stability he might have expected from a dependable income was shattered by a personal blow that saddened him for the rest of his life. His wife, a sickly girl, lost one of two daughters in infancy (a common enough misfortune among Victorians of all classes) and then, in 1840, bore another girl, went insane, and remained so beyond all cure. She stayed on and off with friends in the country and outlived Thackeray. For the next twenty-three years, he remained, as a friend said, "a widower with a wife still alive."

At this distance, it is impossible to say whether this trauma permanently affected his view of life, or whether some such disaster was likely to spring from the character of a man who would choose such a wife. At any rate, he retreated to a club life and slogged away at his hackwork, which he hated except as the least unpleasant way to earn a living. For ten more years, he wrote and collected his random romances, fantasies and facetiae (his *Book of Snobs* gave a

new and lasting meaning to the word) under at least half a dozen pseudonyms. Not until he wrote an historical novel, *The Memoirs of Barry Lyndon,* did he break through into a personal style: a vein of satire tinged with sadism about halfway between Jane Austen and Dickens, too familiar for the one, too elegant for the other. But it was a personal style, and it sent out the first tremors of the volcano that exploded in *Vanity Fair.* By then, he was thirty-six, and the reading public first became aware of William Makepeace Thackeray through his masterpiece, for it was the first work to which he gave his name. This one novel elevated an anonymous essayist and minor satirist into a literary giant, a role he had the modesty and charm never to try to live up to.

In introducing his characters, he playfully pretended that they were puppets at a fair, "not a moral place, certainly not a merry one, though very noisy." But for all its outward gaiety and the rippling elegance of its style, it is almost a tragic work, impossible—in its rich range of characters, and the ambivalence of their motives—to summarize. Enough to say that a huge cast of Regency characters, between the aristocracy and the middle class—grasping merchants, loitering peers, playboys, bankers, wastrels, gamblers, soldiers—does not obscure a nucleus of two types of female and the suitors or victims who swarm about them. And through engagements plotted and broken, marriages, inheritances, disinheritances, gambling sessions and bankruptcies, simple soldiers killed, and calculating soldiers buying their way out of combat, there stalks the immortal Jezebel of Becky Sharp, the antiheroine who, in a moment of self-knowledge, said, "If I had had five thousand a year, I could have been a good woman," and knew she could never make it on ten thousand.

By the time the last parts of *Vanity Fair* were coming out, Thackeray was accused of being a Balzacian cynic. He explained the difference between a cynic and a good novelist:

> I wish to describe men and women, good, bad and indifferent; if they are silly, to laugh at them; if they are good and kindly, to shake them by the hand; if they are wicked, to abuse them. . . . It is not I who, like Miss Sharp, sneers at fidelity . . . it was not I who laughed at the railing old baronet—the laughter comes from one who has no reverence except for prosperity and no eye for anything beyond success. There are people living in the world—faithless, hopeless, charityless. It was to combat and expose such as those, no doubt, that laughter was made.

It is a brave credo, not quite convincing enough to make us forget the settled heartache of his wife's madness, and the gentle stoicism with which it was borne by a man in whom benevolence to everyone around him was his form of courage.

I t has often occurred to me that the only person who might have successfully translated Dickens to the screen is Walt Disney, in his early inventive prime. His characters, too, are built on idiosyncrasy and drawn as beings more alive and less human than humans in the flesh. And when they appear in Disneyland or a Macy's parade, they solidify into walking puppets pretending to be recognizable people, as Dickens's characters do when they are seen as actors of flesh and blood. It seems to me that the only good movie adaptations of Dickens are of those novels—like *Great Expectations* and *A Tale of Two Cities*—in which idiosyncrasy is muted in the interests of a strong melodramatic plot or a conflict between several plain characters. But then, the people who pick *A Tale of Two Cities* as their favorite Dickens novel are proving, by the act of choice, that Dickens is not for them.

Yet Dickens is a ready favorite of directors and writers eager to transfer "the classics" to the screen. Even before the sound film, at least ten of his novels had been made into silent films. A silent Dickens? It is as much of a contradiction as a talkative statue.

The reason for this perverse itch, to dramatize what is least Dickensian about Dickens, is not far to seek. Dickens, like many of his Victorian contemporaries, mined what George Gissing called "the dark underside" of human nature. But it could be made acceptable to the strong propriety of the Victorian reading public by various disguises. We think of Melville passing off a deep human conflict with the sea as a piece of popular adventure, or Lewis Carroll marketing a nightmare by calling it child's play. Most of all, Dickens, who had a quick and merciless sense of the unconscious roots of character, took the curse off it by kidding it in exaggeration, by wildly waving the wand of his comic imagination, by so generously popping the candy of his sentimental sermons into the gaping mouths of the audience he had hypnotized that his admirers were willingly blinded to the very raw material he was feeding them: the murders, seductions, thieveries, extortions, the sadism, miserliness, alcoholism, and ingrown virginity that were his meat. It is the raw material, the lavish opportunities for visual shock, that really attract the dramatizers, while too often the essential Dickens—the great variety of individuals cunningly observed, the feel for what is comic and ironic in human character—goes a-begging.

Our Mutual Friend is ideal for the connoisseur of melodrama. The story of a river rat, a longshoreman who dredges the Thames River for dead bodies and finds a corpse that is identified as the son of a dead man who had made a fortune pulverizing the city's wastes into ash and dust for sale to builders.

67

By the luck of a will whose beneficiary was presumed dead, the inheritance passes to the Cockney foreman for a dust contractor. The brew is thickened by a scoundrel of a river rat who accuses the longshoreman of murder; by a crippled girl who dresses dolls; by a taxidermist ("Preserver of Animals and Birds, and Articulator of Human Bones"); and by the ascent of the Cockney heir into a circle of social climbers. There was enough here to make the television version a fair approximation to what Dickens intended as a story about "the Thames river, passion, money, and dust." As always, much of the social satire—the picture of

Opposite, left: Kind-hearted Mr. Boffin (Leo McKern)
turns miserly after inheriting wealth. Top: John Rokesmith
(John McEnery) and Bella Wilfer (Jane Seymour) find
love. Above and left: Crippled Jenny Wren (Polly James) supports
herself—and alcoholic father—as a doll's dressmaker.

"Dickens's Dream," by R. W. Buss, swarms
with unforgettable creations: Mr. Pickwick, Pip,
and Joe, Oliver, David, Pecksniff, Little
Nell, Barnaby Rudge, the Wellers, Dick Swiveller,
and the Marchioness. Above: Three ages of
Dickens—Boy (Simon Bell), Young Man (Gene Foad),
and triumphant author (Roy Dotrice).

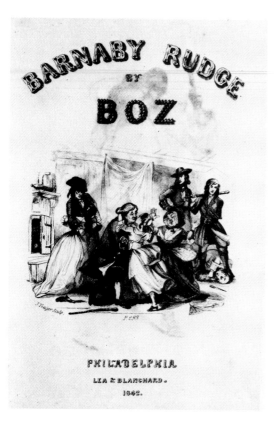

72

the incomparable Veneerings—was lost in pursuit of the labyrinthine plot, which revealed that the drowned man was alive and, indeed, the true heir to the dust fortune.

Dickens of London was a brave attempt, by Yorkshire Television, to dramatize the first thirty-two years of Dickens's life as recalled by Dickens himself on his last reading tour in America. The scriptwriter for the series was novelist Wolf Mankowitz, who made himself a great expert on Dickens (and subsequently published a biography of the author); few Dickensians can have been more conscious of the dramatic problems involved. And the form of the series was an artful way of satisfying one dramatic problem and begging the other. First, Dickens's own early life was full of melodrama. And by limiting the biographical story to the childhood and youth of Dickens, there was no call to parade any of his comic inventions, except in the character of Dickens's father, who was taken—not least by the author himself—to be the inspiration of Mr. Micawber. Also, Dickens's life in America could be offered as a theatrical bonus of special interest to an American audience.

Charles Dickens we saw from his birth in the seaport city of Portsmouth, in 1812, to his first success as a journalist and his first disappointment in love. His father was a clerk in the Navy Pay Office married to a birdbrain who gave her children a little Latin and a lot of affection. The father was a genial, thriftless, verbal dandy escaping his debts in London but not his creditors. He ignored their claims, bought cheaper food, tapped every friend and relation in sight to "raise the wind," but wound up in a debtors' prison. Young Charles was taken out of school and put to work in a malodorous factory capping and labeling pots of shoe-blacking in a murky part of London down by the river. To his protests at losing his education before he'd begun it, his father grandly replied: "What there is to learn can be learned on the streets of London." It was a grim prescription, and nine boys in ten would probably have been emotionally crippled by the squalid company of his daily work, the degradation of visiting his father in prison, and the nightly return to a scraping household in which even the pretense of shabby gentility was a strain. But, from all intimate accounts, he was a lively boy of genial disposition, frail but bristling with animal spirits, and blessed with a genius for observation of people of every sort, degree, and temperament.

Only—in this dramatization—when Dickens was in America for the last time, long separated from his wife, ailing and exhausted, did he come to

73

"Barnaby Rudge" was Dickens's first historical novel. He married
Catherine Hogarth (portrait) and after twenty-two years and ten children
he had a well-hidden affair with Ellen Ternan (photo).
Picture with daughters Mamey and Kate was taken
at Gad's Hill home in 1865, the year of "Our Mutual Friend."

Roy Dotrice as the author's father, John
Dickens, Simon Bell as the boy
Charles, and Diana Coupland as
Mrs. Dickens in scenes from the
biographical "Dickens of London." Father
was Wilkins Micawber to the
life: always charming, always in debt.

74

recognize, in the reflection of the streets of New York and its prisons he visited, the emotional toll that his early years had taken of him. The bloom of youth, Freud once said, anesthetizes many a neurosis. When the bloom has gone, and the flesh shrinks, the nerve ends have to take the strain. Dickens had suffered for nine years from a particular strain not touched on in this series: that of hiding from the world the very existence of his young mistress, Ellen Ternan. (Nobody outside his family and an intimate friend or two ever heard of her until 1938.) Dickens, we have to remember, was not only the most popular novelist of the nineteenth century, acclaimed as the comic genius of the age, he was also a national symbol of the upright, tender, Christian husband. As such, he had started a family magazine called *Household Words*. When the first, and only, rumors of a secret affair were barely broached, he did an extraordinary thing. He devoted a whole editorial in *Household Words* to answering the charges that had never been made. He felt compelled to take his "public" into his confidence over "a personal matter of a domestic and sacredly private character" about which "abominably false rumors" had coupled the separation from his wife with the name of a young lady than whom "upon my soul and honor there is not on this earth a more virtuous and spotless creature."

This strenuous protest satisfied nobody in the know, least of all Dickens. Much later, his favorite daughter wrote: "More tragic and far-reaching in its effect was the association of Charles Dickens and Ellen Ternan and their resultant son than that of Nelson and Lady Hamilton and their daughter. My father was like a madman. . . . Nothing could surpass the misery and unhappiness of our life."

In America, in 1867, Dickens was a fretful, sick man, alternating his usual ferocious bursts of industry with unusually deep bouts of exhaustion. The early American indignation aroused, after his first visit to America, by *Martin Chuzzlewit* and *American Notes* had long cooled. He was once again the beloved, the incomparable Boz. But, depressed by vascular troubles and a heart condition, he was taunted by the conflict between his respectable reputation and the fact. Every generation, I suppose, pays the price of its peculiar neuroses. Dickens was a Victorian pillar and a healthy animal. His editorial in *Household Words* was quite sincere. So was his love for his mistress. This combination makes him, for us, the odd case of a frustrated, passionately sincere Victorian hypocrite. It's not too much to say that the double life broke him.

Above: Father and son make the acquaintance of Mr. Tribe (John Slater). Below: Twelve-year-old Charles goes to work at Warren's Blacking Factory, where he labels and caps pots of shoe black. The wretched boys of the novels are echoes of Dickens's traumatic experience.

*Above: Dickens and his improvident
father enjoy a tankard at a
country tavern. Following "Boz,"
Charles will write the story of
the perambulations of a club
for sporting gentlemen: "The Pickwick
Papers." Faltering at first, it
will become a raging success
with the appearance of Sam Weller.
Right: "Dickens of London"
began with the author, ill with
cold and fever during a triumphant
New York tour, letting his mind
wander a lifetime of memories.
Actor Roy Dotrice played
both John Dickens and
the adult Charles Dickens—
in one memorable
scene, simultaneously.*

There is a good case to be made for calling *Tom Brown's Schooldays* the most popular English novel of the nineteenth century. Hardly a literary masterpiece, it is a classic in the sense that *Uncle Tom's Cabin* is a classic: a novel read by millions who had never read another in their lives, and one that had a profound effect on the social life of the country it is about. For over a hundred and twenty years, it has never been out of print. Well into the 1920s it was still in demand by adults and children who might have heard of *Pickwick* or *Vanity Fair* but would never read either.

It is a remarkable curiosity on several counts. It was the first, and is by now the most-enduring, English schoolboy adventure. It was a rarity in taking for its hero (not a man of blinding fame) a real person and giving him his real name. Since the hero had just become headmaster of Rugby School when the book's author was a small boy there, it is at once an autobiography and a disguised biography. Most oddly, this guileless romp of good boys and wicked boys was conceived as a protest against a school system and against Britain's exploitation of her burgeoning empire.

Its author was an English lawyer, Thomas Hughes, in his mid-thirties and just settled into a happy marriage in Wimbledon when he decided—or a rebellion in India decided him—to pay tribute to his old schoolmaster, dead for fifteen years but already a legendary and controversial pioneer in British education. He was Dr. Thomas Arnold, a classical scholar, Oxford don, and ordained deacon, who, in 1827, at the age of thirty-two, came to a failing boarding school for what we should call the sons of the Establishment. Within fifteen years he had transformed it from a seedy penitentiary for the rich, the near-rich, the sons of the army, the Church, and the City, into the prototype of an English public (i.e., private) school with a mission to train boys for service to the nation at home and abroad. This was an obligation of higher education so taken for granted during the long golden age of the British Empire that it tends today to share the discredit of empires themselves. But Arnold saw, before anybody, the need to begin the training for diplomacy, business, and government in the schools. When he arrived at Rugby, the Napoleonic wars had been over only twelve years. The Empire was still only a loose association of the Canadian colonies, some vast Indian provinces, scattered islands, coaling stations run by voracious trading companies. But there were revolutionary ideas in the air. Within five years, the Reform Act would extend the franchise. Within twelve, the famous Durham Report would propose a radical reform of the colonial system to give the practical running of the colonies into the hands of a homegrown colonial and diplomatic service. Arnold had sniffed these heady ideas. He was certainly the first school-master ever to conceive of a schoolboy elite graduating into national service overseas.

There was nothing casual about Thomas Hughes's decision, thirty years after Arnold began his experiment, to write *Tom Brown's Schooldays* when he did. In 1857, while the British people were applauding the suppression of the Sepoy Rebellion, Hughes was appalled—as he guessed Arnold would have been—at this desperate and bloody native protest against the British East India Company and against a nation whose policies made India a dumping ground for British goods while, by barring Indian manufactures with preposterous tariffs, bankrupting the millions who wove textiles and forcing them to scratch for a living on the arid soil. Parliament saw in the rebellion the dangerous precedent of a local military mutiny. It was, in fact, a national revolt. (Disraeli said so in an unwelcome speech of three hours in the House of Commons. The Prime Min-

80

Scene of Rugby School in 1841. By this time it had
benefitted from a dozen years of Dr. Arnold's progressive
leadership. The haughty young swell taking his ease
is Gerald Flashman (Richard Morant), the bane of Tom's existence
and archetype of the public-school bully.

Top: Good-natured Ned East (Simon Turner) takes Tom
(Anthony Murphy) under his wing. Like Father, like Son:
Supercilious Sir Richard Flashman (Gerald Flood).
Above: Schoolyard fight was part of the initiation of the new boy.
Engraving is of old retainer Thomas Wooldridge.

ister, Lord Palmerston, was quick to reassure Queen Victoria that a "Mr. Campbell, member for Weymouth, who had been many years in India, showed the fallacy of Mr. Disraeli's arguments and the groundlessness of his assertions.")

Hughes, an honest man, would not have publicly proclaimed himself as a man in Arnold's image. He invested his envy and admiration in the printed page and expressed what he took to be his best self in an allegory.

Arnold, played with winning vitality by Iain Cuthbertson, was seen as a man of great sweetness and bounding charm. What is hard for us to discern in him in this play is his originality and imagination. All such schools as Rugby, even the ancient models of Eton and Harrow, taught only Latin and Greek. By way of sport, there was a pack of beagles. The rigid disciplinary code entailed physical punishment from the headmaster and from the whim of the prefects, each with his own boy servant or "fag," a title maintained for another century or more with no sinister or jocular meaning implied. Arnold saw the boys' life as one "of gray tedium relieved by moments of brutality." He announced the radical change of adding mathematics, history, English, and even geography to the curriculum. He was the first public-school headmaster, I believe, to begin to abolish the "fag" system, with its almost irresistible inducements to sadism. Arnold was the first, at least the most notable, of what came to be known as muscular Christians. A resounding preacher, he saw his job as a national stewardship, training the best and the brightest according to God's will to go overseas and lead the blacks and the browns into self-government under the dominion of Our Gracious Queen.

Thomas Hughes became a distinguished judge, but he gave it up to be the leader of a radical group called the Christian Socialists. He sat in Parliament for nine years and introduced one bill, much too inflammatory for the times: a trade-union bill. In his mid-fifties, twenty years after *Tom Brown's Schooldays,* he used the royalties from it to go into the Tennessee mountains and found an experimental colony for dispirited Englishmen "recruited from the ranks of mechanics and tradespeople" and intended for "a reverent and godly life" that would "spread over all the neighboring regions." They did, indeed, "labor with their own hands." They played Rugby football and cricket and started a library. Like many another high-minded commune, they also failed. The place is still called Rugby.

Both Arnold and Hughes were, in our mocking parlance, supreme do-gooders. But, as Hubert Humphrey said: "What's wrong with doing good? Is it better to do bad?"

83

Top: Thomas Hughes (left), whose vastly popular novel
about Tom (right) was a tribute to his own schooling with the
redoubtable reformer Dr. Arnold (below). Cover
painting of Tom en route to Rugby by stagecoach was
for one of many 20th-century American editions.

Thomas Hardy
The Mayor of Casterbridge · Jude the Obscure

In the third century A.D., the Greek critic Longinus laid it down that "the judgment of contemporary work is the last and ripest fruit of much experience." This is impressive until you start to recall the unpredictable fall of reputations dubbed "established" in the obituaries written by the ripest critics: the way in which a writer canonized by one generation is thought paltry or ridiculous by its grandchildren; alternatively, the unsettling frequency with which fly-by-night or "minor" talents—Jane Austen, Hazlitt, Stephen Crane, Pepys, for that matter—become immortalized long after their deaths.

When I was a schoolboy, Thomas Hardy, then in his late eighties, was everywhere thought of as the Grand Old Man of English literature. He was a set piece in school, as well as university, examinations. His ashes were buried in Westminster Abbey and his heart in Dorset, in the parish churchyard of his native town. Within twenty years or so, certainly after the Second World War, he looked like the last of the Victorians and to many people a minor one. According to university teachers in the 1940s and '50s, he bored the young. His works, if not forgotten, were unread. The smart critics protected him from a second and final burial by declaring that his poetry was the thing.

Then, in 1957, the Japanese founded the first Thomas Hardy Society. It took the English ten more years to start their own. At last report, the visitors from the Orient pad diligently round the villages and lands mentioned in the novels. They even learned to brew the drink on which Michael Henchard, the

Thomas Hardy was the last of Britain's 19th-century literary giants. Many—critics and readers alike—have been shocked by his somber, unsentimental novels, with their interest in the creative and destructive power of sex, but his reputation finally is at flood tide.

tragic hero of *The Mayor of Casterbridge,* got drunk. (For the record, it is "furmity," a mix of wheat stewed in milk, raisins, sugar, and spices, and laced with rum. It is served formally at the society meetings in Tokyo and Kyoto.) There is less of a mystery than might at first appear about the Japanese devotion to this intensely English writer. A people that offers five-year courses in the care and training of a shrub, and uses thin wires to teach a tree how to grow, is greatly taken with the accuracy and minuteness of Hardy's descriptions of the Dorset countryside. The Japanese are evidently not squeamish about tragedy. They share his fatalism, which is not surprising. People who have heard much of, or survived, Hiroshima may well be impatient with novels of easy reassurance about the benevolence of nature or the certainty of human happiness. Meanwhile, in the Western world, *Far from the Madding Crowd, The Mayor of Casterbridge,* and *Tess of the D'Urbervilles* have been filmed by the most chic of avant-garde directors.

I doubt that Hardy, this granity, withdrawn character, would have been touched by such cosmopolitan acclaim. He was depressed during his early years in London, uncomfortable there on his later visits. He was a countryman's countryman, born in a Dorset village in 1840, the son of a master mason and a mother whose family had been in Dorset since the fifteenth century. Like everyone around them, they lived by the land and the success or failure of its crops. Hardy went to the village school and on to one in the county seat of Dorchester—the Casterbridge of the novels—and then was articled to an ecclesiastical architect. He read a lot, taught himself Greek, sketched old churches, and at the age of twenty-two took off for London and an architect's apprenticeship. He was good enough to win, within a year or two, a medal from The Royal Institute of British Architects and its annual prize for design. At this point, he was in two minds about his career. He began to write. By an irony he would have been the first to appreciate, his first published piece was a humorous sketch. He fell ill, went into a depression, returned to Dorset, and lived there for the rest of his life.

The Mayor of Casterbridge was his tenth novel, written in his middle forties. He had the idea for it when he was poring over some county records of the 1830s and '40s and came on several advertisements for "wife auctions." He cited these sources when the opening incident of the novel—Henchard's sale of his wife and daughter to a sailor while in a drunken stupor—sent a shock wave through the critics. The story traces, with some pity but no sentimentality, the late return to Casterbridge of Henchard as an anonymous laborer; his moving onwards and upwards to become a thriving wheat and hay

"The Mayor of Casterbridge": Michael Henchard (Alan
Bates) plods the "Wessex" (Dorset) countryside after selling
his wife Susan (Anne Stallybrass) and infant daugher
(middle, right) on impulse to a sailor at
a fair. They reappear years later, when Henchard has
become a wealthy grain merchant and mayor, and his life
is complicated by Lucetta (Anna Massey, below).

merchant and the mayor of Casterbridge; the return of his wife and daughter (who is, in truth, not Henchard's but the sailor's daughter); his unmasking by an old woman who happened to recall the auction; the parading around town of his effigy and that of his mistress; his swift decline into a hired hand; the ultimate humiliation of seeing his "daughter" marry the partner who had annexed first his business and then his mistress; his retreat to a home in a barn; and his death in bitterness and squalor.

The critics complained that in all this there were too many coincidences, too much unlucky circumstance, as in those 1930s movies where a letter slipped over a carpet instead of under it would have saved us from gales of rows,

"Jude the Obscure": Jude Fawley (Robert Powell) and Sue Bridehead (Fiona Walker) are the devoted but mismatched lovers whose aspirations are blighted by character flaws and the twist of circumstances. This was Hardy's last novel. Right: On location.

breast-beating, and recriminations, and, indeed, from the movie itself. Hardy never apologized and never explained. He left it to be inferred that he did not invent coincidences to ease himself out of trouble with tiresome people. His coincidences always arose from a particular weakness of character. He did make the analogy between Oedipus and Henchard: men who tempt the one fate they are most anxious to avoid.

Jude the Obscure was the last of Hardy's novels and his favorite. It is also the most profoundly depressing. In bleakest outline, it is the story of a poor young stonemason who fails to get into Oxford, is seduced by a farm girl who marries and abandons him. When at last he is free to marry his adored cousin, she has sickened of waiting for him and married a schoolmaster. He repels her, and at last the cousin is willing to marry Jude, but on the understanding that their relationship must be celibate, must maintain "a peculiar delicacy which might be ruined if it were intensified." She gives in, and they live in poverty with their two children and his son by the farm girl, a spooky gnome of a child called Little Father Time, who hangs himself and the other children.

It is a bitter choice for a favorite novel. It may be that through it Hardy was expiating his own gray and luckless marriage to a homely, nagging woman who hadn't a clue to his great gifts or the reasons for his fame. However that may be, Hardy, at the age of fifty-four, quit novel-writing and devoted his remaining thirty-four years to lyric poetry, most notably to the immense three-part epic about the Napoleonic wars called *The Dynasts.* In *Jude the Obscure,* he once remarked, he had had his final say about women, "the most vivifying and disturbing influence in human life." By then, nothing so frivolous as a happy ending could ever occur to him. Ten years earlier, he had closed *The Mayor of Casterbridge* with a cautious apology for leaving Henchard's adopted daughter with at least a prospect of happiness:

And in being forced to class herself among the fortunate, she did not cease to wonder at the persistence of the unforeseen, when the one to whom such unbroken tranquility had been accorded in the adult stage was she whose youth had seemed to teach that happiness was but the occasional episode in a general drama of pain.

No wonder Hardy's favorite play was *King Lear.* One sentence in it, by his own admission, summed up his view of character, courage, chance, and circumstance:

> As flies to wanton boys are we to the gods,
> They kill us for their sport.

The delicate inflections of feeling conveyed by the cadences of the line, inflections and cadences which, after so long a course of the ordinary theatrical splashes and daubs of passion and emphasis, are as grateful to my ear as the music of Mozart would be after a year of . . . *Il Trovatore*.

It is Bernard Shaw reviewing Henry James's play, *Guy Domville,* and deploring "the derisive howls from the gallery" that greeted James when he took a curtain call. Five years later, Max Beerbohm reviewed a dramatic adaptation of one of James's stories and, while declaring his love of the exquisite music of Mozart, so to speak, similarly lamented that "of all that I love in Mr. James's mind, so very little can be translated into the sphere of drama." Between them Shaw and Beerbohm probably produced the only sympathetic criticisms of James, as dramatist, Max saying, however, that the dialogue was too finely spun for the theatre, Shaw saying that it constituted pearls tossed at the swine of the Victorian audience.

James's yearning to be a successful dramatist overcame him at a time, in his late forties, when he felt he had exhausted two rich veins of gifts as a novelist. He was born in 1843, a New Yorker, the grandson of an Irish immigrant who amassed a fortune, and the son of a religious visionary. Like his brother William (to become the father of modern psychology), he was shuttled back and forth across the Atlantic, receiving no settled education. Both of them attended, at irregular intervals, schools in the United States, France, and Switzerland, and in his youth Henry took leisurely tours of England, France, and Italy.

It was an education providentially suited to the peculiar talents of Henry James. He happened to possess a set of antennae for observing the rich, the near-rich, the genteel, and the climbers finer than anything that had been seen in the English or American novel up to that time, and his travels sharpened them. One year before he settled for good in London, when he was thirty-three, he began to mine, in short stories and novels, his first and richest vein: the suppressed tension that always exists between the manners and values of cultivated Americans and Europeans, in particular the conflict between the visiting American (women, usually), innocent but self-reliant, and the European, corrupt but wise. In the 1880s, feeling that he had temporarily exhausted this vein, he returned to two American themes: one, in *The Bostonian*, setting a manly, traditional Southerner against an almost paranoid Boston suffragette; the other, in *The Princess Casa-*

massima, about a young man attracted to the idea of revolution and exhausted by it.

For the next five years, he wrote for the stage, with the wounding results we have noted. James's exquisite probing of manners and motives, of passions curbed by the delicate but firm reins of convention, could not be amplified to the large, grandiloquent scale of the Victorian-Edwardian theatre. It was chamber music for the wrong theatre at the wrong time.

I have gone into this unhappy episode in James's life because it is crucial to the adaptation of this work for television. And it is a curious and happy fact that his calm and wary analysis of the emotions of people who on the surface

*Henry James (top left) and classic creations: Amerigo
(Daniel Massey) and Charlotte (Gayle Hunnicutt) at top
right, Maggie (Jill Townsend) and Adam Verver (Barry Morse),
all from "The Golden Bowl"; Fleda Vetch (Gemma Jones) and
Mrs. Gereth (Pauline Jameson), in "The Spoils of Poynton."*

appear to be impeccably correct is just what the small screen craves. Television is not so much a miniature theatre as a powerful microscope for scanning the emotions concealed under gestures so small as a licked lip (Jimmy Carter) or a defensive chuckle (Ronald Reagan). It is an ideal medium for Henry James, who could make a polite refusal to take a walk a turning point in a long friendship, and a raised eyebrow more ominous than an earthquake. There remains, however, the relevance of Beerbohm's complaint about James's elaborate dialogue, a literal translation of everything, the essential and the unessential, that people would use in real life. But, wrote Beerbohm, "style in [theatre] dialogue is a matter of compression from real life, never of translation." Luckily, Jack Pulman, the adapter for these dramas, was alive to this distinction and was on hand as the compressor and distiller.

As often in the later James, these stories have bare plots and are ideal for the new medium. They have the right scale, they spring from no large events but from the recollection of passing remarks at a dinner table. Here, for instance, James has told us how *The Spoils of Poynton* came about:

One Christmas Eve, when I was dining with friends, a lady beside me made, in the course of the talk, one of those allusions that I have always found myself recognizing on the spot as a "germ" . . . she spoke of a good lady in the North [of England] who was at daggers drawn with her only son . . . over the ownership of the valuable furniture of a fine old house just accruing to the young man by his father's death . . . she spoke but ten words, yet I recognized in a flash all the possibilities of the little drama of my Spoils.

He shut his ears to what he called "the futility of fact" and allowed the incident to ferment in his mind. A dozen years later, it had mellowed into a vintage product. The spoils are the furniture and other precious objects lovingly collected by a mother whose house, Poynton, has been willed to her son by his father. The son is about to marry a muscular deb, a philistine in all matters of art off the tennis court. The mother gives up the house but takes all its spoils and installs them in a smaller house to which she invites a Miss Vetch, a sensitive mouse of a girl of great taste. The son pleads with this girl to help him get back the spoils, and in so doing falls in love with her, and she with him. But at the back of his dim mind, along with other misgivings, is the prospect of a breach-of-promise suit. James wrote in his preface to this work that "all drama centers round a battle between a collection of fools and one free spirit." Miss Vetch is that free spirit. In renouncing the son and committing herself to spinsterhood, she is not, in James's eyes, an object of pathos. She exemplifies what for him was "the one great human virtue: renunciation."

The Golden Bowl, the last—and some think the finest—of his novels, has a plot as spare as any he conceived. An American, a millionaire art collector, has an adored daughter, Maggie, who is married to an impoverished Italian prince. The father is married to Charlotte, a childhood friend of his daughter's. As the marriages seem to settle into a placid routine, the prince and Charlotte begin to see too much of each other and run the risk of disclosing the knowledge that long ago they had been lovers. The crucial detail of the plot is a golden bowl that Maggie has gone to buy as a birthday present for her father. And the fateful revelation comes from the shopkeeper who sold it. On delivering it to Maggie's house, he notices two photographs—one of the prince and one of Charlotte—and he drops the casual remark that four years ago, on the eve of Maggie's wedding, Charlotte had stopped in his shop and would have bought the bowl for the prince if it had not been cracked. In James, a shopkeeper's remark is all that is needed to shatter four lives. (James's favorite device, of using the novelist's prose not to tell *us* what to think but to explain what the characters are thinking behind the mask of their behavior, was brilliantly adopted in this television version by Cyril Cusack, stepping into the play as a friend and out of it as the novelist.)

H. L. Mencken once made the curious, and surely debatable, remark that if James had stayed in his own country and gone west, instead of east, he would have come on the life of the frontier "and in meeting it would have become as great an artist as Mark Twain." This thought seems to suggest that James was spoiled for want of vital material. It presupposes a theory of emotional toughness wholly at war with James's instincts, a hypothesis that the raw material of a great storyteller must lie in primitive emotions simply expressed in characters confronting the elemental means of life. James did not need to look into a volcano to be moved. He heard volcanoes rumbling beneath the most genteel social behavior.

There is a revealing story about him. He was staying once, in the 1890s, in an English country house when the only child of a neighbor died of a sudden illness. James had recently quarrelled with the neighbor and was not on speaking terms with him. He decided, nevertheless, to attend the funeral. His host tried to dissuade him; it might stir up bad blood, there was no need to make an effort to be courteous. Courtesy was not the point. James went, and when he returned his host asked him how he could have brought himself to sit in the pew just behind the mourning family. James looked piercingly at his host. He said: "Where emotion is, there am I." A very tough gentleman, as tough as any frontiersman.

Except to the student of British political history, and perhaps even to him, the abiding interest in Disraeli must be psychological. How could a Jew, a quarter century before racial and social prejudices had been tamed sufficiently to allow Jews to sit in the House of Commons, think of entering British politics? How did it happen that a conceited young fop, a blatant outsider, could come to have great landowners, stolid farmers, gifted statesmen, the cream of the English aristocracy, at his beck and call? And how could a fawning climber obsessed with society and its ceremonies develop a passionate concern for the laboring poor and lead the Conservative party, of all complacent establishments, into doing something about it?

He was born in London in 1804, when most of the Jews of Europe were living in a dark age. Only in France had the Revolution given them the vote. In England, they were barred from the professions and the universities and from most crafts, and they could not hold government office of any kind. Granting this, there are people who will claim that Disraeli was a special and fortunate case, that his father, a Jew of Italian descent, was a wealthy scholar, an eminent collector of curiosities of literature, a gentle self-effacing man who, not least, had effaced what were then taken to be the obvious characteristics of his race. And more, that Disraeli's mother was a descendant either of one of the ancient Portuguese families or of a distinguished Sephardic family run out of Spain at the end of the fifteenth century. Disraeli ornamented this escutcheon later on, but it has been proved to be a total fantasy, gradually created in the mind of the young Disraeli possibly to prove to himself that in aspiring to the English nobility he was simply recovering his heritage. The religious fact would seem to have been an insuperable obstacle. It was removed not by Disraeli but by the lucky accident of a quarrel his father had with the rabbi of their Sephardic synagogue, which led him to remove his children and to have them baptized as Christians.

The young Disraeli was a listless scholar who took only to Latin and to his father's library. Very soon he became, to put it mildly, a family nuisance and a chronic burden to his father. He lived high, he curled his hair in decorative coils, like a stage Levantine, he dressed with absurd garishness, his hands a-dazzle with rings. He fancied himself a speculator and failed disastrously with mining stock. He nudged his father to persuade a friend to start a newspaper, to which the twenty-one-year-old Disraeli promised a capital share. The paper failed, and Disraeli welshed on his share. Together, these losses loaded him with debts for the next thirty-odd years.

Apparently untouched by conscience, he continued to live at home, to make peacock appearances in any society that would tolerate him, and he

In the anti-Semitic Britain of
the 1820s, Benjamin Disraeli (Ian
McShane) cut an outlandish
figure as a dandy.
He had the effrontery
to enter politics, but emerged as
a statesman of skill and power
and a trusted friend of his queen,
who made him Earl of Beaconsfield.
He helped Victoria survive the
trauma of Albert's death and
succeeded in acquiring
the Suez Canal for Britain.

"NEW CROWNS FOR OLD ONES!"

Top: McShane's flamboyant Disraeli. The real one played himself at least as broadly. Famous photograph shows a relaxed "Dizzy" in velvet jacket. Cartoon comments on his Oriental guile in persuading Victoria to become empress of India, an imperial responsibility opposed in Britain.

decided, as one might decide to take up riding, to become a novelist. He wrote a huge novel and burned it. He wrote another, published anonymously, in five volumes, called *Vivian Grey,* which cruelly satirized the failed publisher he had welshed on but also presented a fanciful picture of high society. In spite of turgid descriptions and stilted dialogue, the critics praised it highly until they discovered that it had been written by a middle-class Jew, very soon identified as the publisher's debtor. However, on the score of this small success, he received an advance for another novel, traveled abroad on it; his health broke, and he went into depression. He returned to London, wrote the novel, and got a handsome advance on the next one. This time, he took off on a sixteen-month tour of Eastern Europe, going through Spain, Greece, Albania, Egypt, and Jerusalem. Everywhere he went, he added some article of native dress to his costume. Everywhere, he reported back home, he astonished the natives: "The people made way for me as I passed, it was like the opening of the Red Sea."

Everything in his behavior between his late teens and his middle twenties strongly suggests a character strutting in dreamland if not blithely poised on the edge of insanity. Certainly today his depressions, his acting-out of delusions of grandeur, his lack of conscience toward his benefactors, would likely be ascribed to a psychopathic personality.

However, on his second trip abroad he had with him as a traveling companion the fiancé of his adored sister (she seems to have represented his one rock of sympathy in an antipathetic world, and he repaid her affection with lifelong devotion). The fiancé died quite suddenly of smallpox. This shocked and steadied him like nothing that had happened before. He came home again, to drop a mistress and take a mistress and to make the remarkable decision to enter politics.

But as what? Even though he had been admitted, if only as a witty eccentric, into some fashionable literary salons, even though there were political habitués who saw through the dandyism into the makings of an orator, he had no political attachments, let alone a political base. His approaches to the leader of the Tories, Sir Robert Peel, were snubbed. He hated the liberal Whigs. His family had moved into a house in Buckinghamshire, and there, in a county constituency, of all unlikely places, he chose to stand as an independent radical. The franchise was then severely limited to electors handpicked by the county squires and landowners. A young and flashy Jew was the last person qualified to make up to them, and he hadn't the money to bribe them. He lost. Twice in the next three years he stood again, and twice more he lost. Obviously, he had to modify his political colors, if not—for some more years—his costume. Reluc-

97

tantly, he joined the Tory Conservatives, stood, and lost again. But he had something to offer, especially to a strong Conservative faction that bridled at many of Peel's policies and his paternal grip on the party. What Disraeli could bring to these dissidents was a gift of florid invective. He put out some withering manifestoes, mostly against the Conservative government itself, and he began to attract attention as a bizarre cuckoo in the nest: a novel combination of a royalist and a populist, an ardent advocate of the Army, the Crown, the Empire, and the Church, but the scourge of both parties for what he called their "aristocratic neglect" of working people. It was a strange new theory. It was the first blast of what came to be known as "Tory Democracy."

On his fifth try as a parliamentary candidate, he was financed by a wealthy Conservative, Wyndham Lewis, and he won. It was 1837, the year of Victoria's accession. He was thirty-three.

His maiden speech was everything his detractors could have wished: pretentious, absurdly literary, egotistical. He was laughed at, he was booed, he was shouted down. He withdrew with the famous, true line: "I will sit down now but the time will come when you will hear me." It took some years for even his political friends to credit him with a promising political career. He did begin to temper his florid style and accommodate his impulsiveness to the patient tactics of the House. But he was still a Jew at a time when anti-Semitism among top people was nothing muttered behind the palm of the hand. He had fearful

Mrs. Wyndham Lewis (portrait) was the
wife of Disraeli's first political sponsor. She was fifteen
years his senior and he thought she was
a dunce, but he married her when Lewis died.
The actress Mary Peach (left) played her.

his Jewishness nor flaunted it defiantly. He adopted rather the role of a distinguished exotic, like that of an Indian prince, a rare and valuable variation on the
English patriot, and he trusted to the English familiarity with eccentrics to accept
him at his valuation.

However subtle and devious he had been in acquiring power,
throughout the rest of his political life he hammered away at a few rooted
convictions, though they were unpopular with the Tory right wing and anathema
to the Liberals: to build up the small and derided British army so that it counted
for something on the Continent as a deterrent to European wars; to forbid its
being used to discipline the Irish rebels; to press a grand plan for clearing the
slums of London and cleansing the industrial cities of their stinking pollution;
above all, to give the working people of the towns the vote, no matter how much
Gladstone might deplore the idea as "an invitation to mob rule." This last appeal
made Disraeli, at last, Prime Minister, but for only a few months. He had spent
over thirty years in opposition, trying and failing to meld the right and left wings
of the Conservatives. When, after six more years, he became Prime Minister for
the second time, he was seventy and his health steadily failed him throughout
the six years of his administration. It was too late, and he was too ill to cap a
lifetime of rebellion with a sustained run of achievement. All the best of him had
been spent in humanizing the Conservatives and broadening their foreign hori-
zons.

There is probably no other Victorian Englishman, and few politicians
of any time, whose essential character was so much disputed in his own time. To
his political enemy Gladstone, he was "a schemer and a charlatan." To the Prime
Minister who succeeded him, he was "a model of patience and gentleness and
unswerving loyalty." To Queen Victoria, once he was in office, "a dear and valued
friend." To Thomas Carlyle he was "not worth his weight in cold bacon."

He was most likely one and all of these things, to different people
at different times. His achievement as a man is no more and no less than that of
one who in middle age managed a slow and arduous triumph over flaws of
character that would have ruined an ungifted man early in life. As an achievement
of statesmanship, it was his daring conception of Tory democracy and his relentless concern for the working classes that gave the Conservative party a decent
rationale in its lean years and, better, a rightful claim to move into the twentieth
century as a formidable party. Since Disraeli, the Conservatives have not had a
leader with such insight into the way things, in Britain at any rate, were bound
to go.

Part 3

Nineteenth-Century Giants:
The Continentals

Honoré Balzac
Père Goriot   Cousin Bette

There were only three French writers whose novels were dramatized for our television theatre. But they were among the great ones, and Balzac is the greatest. In the growth of the French novel, they are so plainly offspring of one another that if the transmission of genius were as direct as the Eugenists once hoped, Flaubert would be the son of Balzac and Zola would be the grandson.

Their lives precisely span a century, the nineteenth, which saw French fiction forsake its transplantings from Spain and England and Germany and find its own roots in contemporary French life. Only thirty years before Balzac was born, the regular form of the French novel was a sequence of letters, philosophical or satirical, emotional only to the extent that they examined the soul of the author: for the most part, essays in the expression of what the eighteenth century prized more than realism or compassion or moralizing—what it called "sensibility." It is customary to say that after Goethe appeared in French translation, in 1776, the subsequent spate of fictional memoirs, recounting with dogged introspection the splendors and—mostly—the miseries of the human ego, sounded the first approach of Romanticism. Romanticism might have come charging in to overwhelm the prevailing fashion if it had not been arrested by the most tremendous event in French history. For between the *Confessions* of Rousseau and the first light of Balzac's work arose the barricades of the Revolution, which very soon imprisoned the liberties it had lately released, intimidated the imagination of writers, drove Chateaubriand into exile (a pensive Solzhenitsyn contemplating the Indians near Niagara Falls), and put a premium on party manifestoes and hacks writing obediently under police supervision.

Balzac was lucky to have been born ten years after the Revolution (he was also lucky to die just before the tyranny of the Second Empire). If he had been born thirty years earlier, his insight into the characters of the revolutionaries, and the suppression of his volcanic energy, might have been the end of him.

Honoré Balzac (the "de" was an inventive flourish added when he went up in the world) was born in Tours, in 1799, of a long line of laborers and peasants, but his father managed to push his way up into the commissary department of the army. The son was subjected to the most dogmatic kind of French upbringing: put out to nurse, sent at the age of seven to a grammar school as a boarder, and denied all holidays. His father, a self-made fugitive from the working class, was resolved that his son should not retreat into it. He must study the law, which he did assiduously, and practice it, which he refused to. His

A man of great energy, Balzac wrote 142 volumes,
and is recognized as France's greatest novelist. Photography,
invented in the last decade of his life, evidently
did him justice. Of this daguerreotype he wrote: "What is
admirable is its truthfulness and its precision!"

father accordingly put him in a garret on a minute allowance in the hope of starving him into obedience. It didn't work. Instead, he sat down in his miserable lodgings and wrote a tragedy and, in the next five years, fifteen novels, innumerable essays, parodies, romances, thrillers, melodramas; none of them, he decided, much good, none of them signed, none of them thought fit to be admitted later to his collected works. He could not earn a living from them, but he appears not to have been embittered by the enormous industry they involved.

He turned to business, tried printing, publishing (on money borrowed either from his mother or from one or another of two ladies of the liberal bourgeoisie), and in his twenty-ninth year bought a type foundry. It failed, and on an initial indebtedness of 60,000 francs he built a monument of debt that shadowed him and exasperated him for the rest of his life, but in which he took an almost scornful pride. He might declare on sober days that debt was the great destroyer of friendship and the chief inducement to crime. His novels were to elaborate mercilessly on this theme. But he was nothing like so harsh on himself as he was on his characters. Once he had made a small name, he lived and dressed

The wealth of characters inhabiting "Père Goriot" are among the two thousand Balzac created for his "Comédie Humaine." Left: Michael Goodliffe as doting Père Goriot, David Dundas as vain, ambitious Eugène de Rastignac. Right: Residents of Mme. Vauquer's boardinghouse.

in showy defiance of his creditors. He once wrote, and often quoted: "A debt is a work of the imagination which no tax collector can understand."

Almost all this early work was unfruitful only in the sense of being imitative, not about the life he knew. It was a five-year exercise in pastiche from a wide range of models, including Scott, Byron, Rousseau, and even Fenimore Cooper. Much of it infused with romantic recall of the Napoleonic days by somebody who wasn't there. But, through high-born female patrons and the access they gave him to a society sunning itself in the restoration of the monarchy, he looked around him—at the salons and in the streets—and wrote his first signed work, a two-volume novel about the drain that desire puts on a man's energies. It is a moral, not to say a puritanical, theme. But so are the themes of most of Balzac's novels. They are saved at every turn from being moral tracts by the penetrating candor of his observation of life as it is.

At last having a name he could flourish before the literary world, he now set himself a task, a planned body of work, as systematically as the young John D. Rockefeller planned to create an oil industry. He calculated that his survey of the whole of French society, no less—from its alley cats through its trades and professions and on up through its galloping plutocracy to the desiccated aristocracy—would require between two and three thousand characters (the final figure, computed by some mole of a scholar, was 2,472, with 566 unnamed characters). He would adopt a working routine of fifteen hours a day. He would write continuously a vast series of novels, 142 in all. As it was, in the twenty years remaining to him, he published ninety-one novels, twenty of them in the first three years. He gave the whole output the general title of *The Human Comedy*.

Père Goriot is one of the earliest novels, written when Balzac was thirty-five, and *Cousin Bette* is one of the last, written four years before his death. Goriot is an old, once rich man who has squandered every sou in trying to buy for his two bloodsucking daughters a place in society. Merely the most tragic consequence of this hectic ambition is to put one of the daughters beyond the reach of a poor, decent law student and involve him in adultery, bankruptcy, and murder. "Nothing more," wrote Balzac, "than an account of what happens to people who insist on keeping up appearances."

Cousin Bette has a parallel theme. She is the poor relation of a rich baron, a vain, charming womanizer. The happiest and most generous thing she has done in her life is to befriend a poor sculptor and give him a room in her shabby apartment. However, he falls in love with the Baron's daughter, and Cousin Bette—crushed by the loss of her only intimate relationship—devotes all

105

her anger and ingenuity to a series of revenges, plotted not against the daughter but against the Baron himself. She baits him with the dissolute young wife of a lowly clerk in the War Office, where the Baron heads a department. The Baron sets this woman up as his mistress, and, in his increasingly vain efforts to counter the advances of three other lovers, he bankrupts himself, disgraces the clerk, and impoverishes his wife. Still pathetically trying to keep the girl as his sole possession, the Baron enlists an uncle in an embezzlement scheme and sees the man shoot himself. The Baron goes into hiding and leaves his wife in the care of his son, who is discovered to be yet another lover of his father's mistress.

Until the end of his life, Balzac lived in a France in gross reaction against the Revolution: a febrile society, corrupt, money-mad, dominated by a bourgeoisie whose motto—literally coined by a statesman and historian of the time—was "get rich quick." Many faded revolutionaries, disillusioned liberals, and simply decent old men, lamented in the France of the 1830s and '40s what Mark Twain was to lament in the America of the 1870s: "an era of incredible rottenness." Balzac was not one of them. He found in this feverish society all the

material he needed. He was a voluble and opinionated man but, unlike those earnest avant-garde playwrights who tell us at tortured length how we should think and feel about their work, he wasted no words on saying what he was doing in any particular novel. He left the reader to discover its complexities. He saw himself as an objective pathologist of a society driven by "money, power, flattery, greed, ambition." But his confidence in this role, the intensity of his belief in knowing what he was doing, implies a moral vision that sees always the possibility of goodness. It is true, as a famous English lady complained, that Balzac's characters are "all really dreadful people." So are the characters of Dante's *Inferno*.

The sustained, the unparallelled, effort of turning out over ninety-one novels in twenty years, and in the waking hours left to him of conducting much correspondence and many love affairs, was too much for him. His great bulk collapsed at the age of fifty-one. No photograph catches more than a glimpse of the banked fires and writhing energies of this Titan, but they are frozen for us once and for all in the towering statue of him by Rodin.

Cousin Bette: Margaret Tyzack (above) is the vengeful spinster whose intrigues destroy the Hulot family. Colin Baker is Steinbock, the young artist. Opposite: Baron Hulot (Thorley Walters) is the elderly roué whose inability to control his impulses gives Bette her chance at revenge.

George Sand
Notorious Woman

Georgie Sand is one of those historical characters—Schubert, Disraeli, Lincoln, Cleopatra, Lola Montez are others—who live by the legend of their characters more than their works. They are sacred or scandalous or sentimental puppets in a pantheon of the famous and the infamous. Not the least of their attractions is that they do not require the ordinary citizen to know much about their lives. Indeed, he instinctively senses that to poke behind the façade into the facts might destroy the picture of them that we all keep at the back of our minds. In a sense that Oscar Wilde probably didn't intend, it is true of them that "ignorance is like a delicate fruit. Touch it, and the bloom is gone."

There was enough lurid behavior in George Sand to have made her the queen of the gossip columns at any time. In her time, she made a point of being the arch-shocker of the bourgeoisie. And so she is an irresistible magnet to actresses. In the 1930s, Marlene Dietrich had no sooner caused palpitations in the press by appearing in public in slacks than the idea occurred to someone that George Sand had gone further: she dressed for much of her life in men's clothes. So Merle Oberon played George Sand.

Today, it has been discovered that George Sand was the first eminent woman journalist, battled the male literary establishment of Paris, and actually talked about the "rights" of women. What are we waiting for? Why have we been so blind all these years? Surely, she was the indomitable pioneer of feminism. She wasn't, but the reminder that a century or more ago, some woman had resented the rights of men—especially over women in marriage—was enough to revive her gutsy life in a palatable dramatic form.

She was baptized in Paris, in 1804, with the impressive name of Amandine Aurore Lucie Dupin Dudevant. Her mother, an on-and-off prostitute who married a month before she gave birth, was the daughter of a bird-fancier. Her father was the soldier son of an illegitimate mother with direct, but illegitimate, lines running through to Augustus the Second of Poland. Aurore (George Sand) was a girl of high birth and low breeding.

She was brought up by her grandmother in the farming country of Berry, southwest of the Loire, where—in the intervals of a convent schooling—she hunted and rode, married a weak husband, and after a vigorous affair with a free-thinking, freewheeling neighbor took off for Paris. She broke into journalism, and quickly into novels, made a symbolic protest against the male dominance of the publishing world by dressing in men's clothes, and adopted the male pseudonym of George Sand. She pledged herself in turn to a series of lovers

*Drawing by the French artist Garvani emphasizes
the men's clothes Sand liked to wear, but gives her doll-like
features she did not have. In an age of inequality
between the sexes, she enjoyed complete personal freedom and
found friends and lovers among Paris's intellectual elite.*

and the literary or political movements they championed: to the Romantic movement in literature, to Socialism, reincarnation, republicanism, but never to Balzac's or Flaubert's ideas about realism. ("You aim at painting people as they are, I am inclined to paint them as I wish they were.") It was a rousing time for a crusader, and in France, certainly, variety was the spice of revolution. She was born only months before Napoleon took the crown from the hands of the Pope and made himself emperor. She was eleven when the Battle of Waterloo was fought and the monarchy restored. She endured and applauded the workers' revolution of 1830, she lived through the revolution of 1848, the Second Empire, the siege of Paris in 1870, and the beginning of the Third Republic.

Although she came to be thought of as the archetypical Bohemian (after Henri Murger, in his novel *Scènes de la Vie de Bohème,* had coined the word), she was too tough at the core, too independent, to embrace for long either one lover or the cause he espoused.

The important thing about her, which the glitter and turbulence of her private life eclipses, was her work: the product of a writer of original talent and unfaltering industry. Her early novel *Valentine* should have reminded her urban circle from the beginning that she was at bottom a countrywoman seduced, though for the longest time, by the metropolis. It was, as many of her novels were to be, about peasants and farmers in her native region. It was at once

111

Men in her life: Sand (Rosemary Harris, opposite)
broke with "littérateur" Prosper Mérimée (Alan Howard) because he
was too violent, lavished years of care and affection on
Chopin (George Chakiris, above). Liszt (drawing), who
collected women, thought her a heartless collector of men.

acclaimed as a masterpiece by Balzac and Sainte-Beuve. Thereafter, in spite of her serial liaisons with Musset, Mérimée, Chopin, and various lawyers, journalists, and musicians, she continued with clockwork precision to turn out novels, eighty of them, always working from midnight till four a.m., sometimes ending one novel as the night faded and starting another as the dawn came in. Very many have workmen or farmers for heroes, strong, simple idealists working, loving, and dying in the Berry country that was to the end her true literary landscape. The long neglect of her writings, which set in soon after her death and is probably now complete, can be attributed to the betrayal of her Parisian legend by her subject matter. The sort of sophisticated reader likely to be attracted to her name is apt to be put off to find himself up to his knees in a spring thaw and the preoccupations of cattle breeders.

As for her reputation as a feminist, that is obviously the bait which tempted the television producers. And the danger here is that which any dramatist runs who delves into the past: that of imposing our values on the period and its people, and making George Sand come out as Germaine Greer or Betty Friedan. As a pedestrian fact, Sand's contemporaries, principally John Stuart Mill and Miss Emily Davies can be said to have launched a "movement" (one amongst others) for the enfranchisement and emancipation of women from their legal and social inequalities. George Sand led no organized crusade, sponsored no movement, but the early problems with her divorce, and the barricade of male prejudice she found herself up against in the Paris literary world, provoked her to explode often enough into language that at least can be seen as a counterpoint to some of the current arguments of feminism. In this, Flaubert confessed himself sufficiently shocked and enlightened to say that she was a hundred years ahead of her time.

The cosmetic that seals and beautifies her legend is, of course, that of her physical appearance. Such an erotic legend is doomed always to be represented by a gleaming beauty groaning with passion and heaving with jealousy. I know of no record of her having been played by any woman less than handsome. Merle Oberon was an exquisite Oriental butterfly, physically and temperamentally about as far removed from the original as it is possible to conceive. Rosemary Harris was a more solid beauty. However, we have an eyewitness to George Sand's physical charms, a man who was at all times very susceptible to female beauty. When Charles Dickens was living for a year or so in Paris in the mid-1850s, George Sand was fifty-one. He asked to meet her and she herself set "the day and the hour for this interesting festival." He enjoyed the evening. She was opinionated but "in a quiet and agreeable way." But he found it hard "to imagine

anybody more unlike my preconceptions than the illustrious Sand. Just the kind of woman in appearance whom you might suppose to be the Queen's monthly nurse. Chubby, matronly, swarthy, black-eyed . . . a singularly ordinary woman in appearance and manner."

If her life had to be summarized truly in capsule form, we could say: plain child of a lowborn mother and highborn father, a tomboy who grew impatient with a weak husband, decamped to Paris, became a journalist and novelist under the guise of a male pen name, and was intermittently a revolutionary Socialist. She was the mistress of many famous men, and a guilty one, since she had a lifelong hankering after fidelity. When she found an approximation to the perfect mate that never was, she smothered him in care and affection, staying eight years with Chopin and fourteen years with a tubercular engraver. Like most ardent radicals, she was a puritan who reverted, for the last twenty years or so of her life, to a strict conservatism and a niggling concern for the social proprieties. A ferocious worker, she wrote over a hundred books, most of which have gone long unread, including all her best work, a positive library of bucolics that show her steady understanding of the poor and a loving knowledge of trees, fruits, flowers, farms, crops, and landscape as accurate if not as deep as that of Thomas Hardy.

Like most actresses who have played Sand, Rosemary Harris is delightfully more attractive than the reality—as the bewigged portrait by Nadar proves. Louis Napoleon described her as possessing "a man's qualities without a man's faults."

Gustave Flaubert
Madame Bovary

Madame Bovary has been written about more than any other novel of the past hundred years. At the last count, there were over five thousand studies of it, character by character, scene by scene, motive by motive, sentence by sentence. From Baudelaire to Jean-Paul Sartre, it has been dismembered and put together again, and for all the babel of argument about it, everyone agrees it is a masterpiece.

When it came out, in 1856, the most influential of French critics, Sainte-Beuve, wondered that anyone could be engrossed by a story about "the most hackneyed possible setting, the French countryside; the dullest people, the ordinary people of a country town; and the most over-worked theme in literature, adultery." Well, whatever there may be in *Madame Bovary* that ensnares generation after generation, there is no doubt about what prompted its original success. Flaubert was prosecuted on the ground of the novel's immorality, which would have been an odd and astonishing assertion of virtue on the part of the upper-middle-class plutocracy of Balzac's France, but that France had, within a year of Balzac's death, suffered an upheaval.

The scrupulous Flaubert (above) took four years
to write "Madame Bovary," and he was promptly prosecuted by
the French government for "immorality."
Opposite: Emma (Francesca Annis), Charles (Tom Conti), her
husband, and Rodolphe (Denis Lill), her lover.

In 1848, the monarchy of Louis Philippe, grown intolerable to the urban proletariat, was overthrown and the nephew of Napoleon Bonaparte was elected president of the Second Republic. Within three years, he had gained control of the army and, in a military coup, proclaimed himself dictator of France. On the promise of restoring the vote to the poor, he was overwhelmingly confirmed in a national plebiscite. One year later, he called for another plebiscite, which ratified his chosen new title as Emperor of the French. So, in 1852, France succumbed to the tyranny of the Second Empire, under Napoleon the Third, who, among other Draconian measures, barred Republicans from voting, throttled the press, and restored the censorship of literature. Four years later, *Madame Bovary* was published, and its author was brought to trial. To the vast majority of its readers, Flaubert's was a new name, a talent that had bloomed late, for peculiar reasons of his character, and the tyrannical working conditions it imposed on him.

Gustave Flaubert was born in Rouen, in 1821. His father was a distinguished surgeon married to a doctor's daughter. The son was sent to Paris to study law, but two years later he came down with what was called a "nervous disease," which was with him for the rest of his life. It was cautiously diagnosed as epilepsy, perhaps because of honest bafflement, more likely because of the popular stigma that attached—and has continued to attach—to epileptics. (Since the recent and valuable work done on epilepsy—and the dawning suspicion that on the whole epileptics tend to be more intelligent and gifted than most—it seems likely that Flaubert was, in fact, an epileptic.) At any rate, he broke off his law studies. A year or two later, both his father and sister died. At the age of twenty-five, he retired with his mother to the family estate near Rouen, on the Seine, where he lived for most of his life.

He had been a scribbler since his teens, and for twenty years or so he wrote incessantly. "Incessantly" is maybe the wrong word, since it suggests the driven, headlong routine of Balzac. No writer was ever so ordered, or fastidious, or self-critical as Flaubert. At the age of sixteen, he finished a manuscript that was, in essence, the first draft of a *Sentimental Education,* which would be completely rewritten twice more before he let it be published, when he was forty-eight. Similarly, when he was eighteen, he started what he conceived as a French *Faust.* It was to be called *The Temptation of St. Anthony.* He took it up again seven years later and labored over it for three years, at last reading it over to two friendly writers, who deplored its mystical lyricism, urged him to burn it, and suggested he turn to some more earthy temptation. A recent newspaper scandal

was suggested: the heartbreak of a country doctor over his wife's infidelity. A friend of Flaubert's had suffered a similar misfortune. From one, or both, of these stories he conceived the story of *Madame Bovary*. After his only foreign excursion—a six-month trek through Egypt, Palestine, Turkey, Greece, and Italy—he came home to Rouen and worked for four years on *Madame Bovary*. (*The Temptation of St. Anthony* was alternately shelved and worked on for the next twenty odd years and published when he was fifty-three, only six years before his death.)

What was there in Flaubert, of excessive indecision or a neurotic quest for perfection, that compelled him to work for thirty-two years on one proposed masterpiece, and thirty-five years on another, before he would let them be published? He would have had a calm answer, which does, however, bypass the question. He admitted that writing was "an anguish" but he could not let a word or a sentence stand until he had found for it the exact expression. ("There are no such things," he used to say, "as synonyms.") He settled to his round table every morning with his papers primly arranged. He wrote for five or six hours. He paused, for hours, sometimes for days, for the proper word or cadence. One good sentence a day he regarded as work well done. He would have agreed

"It was a substantial-looking farm." So wrote Flaubert
of the real house, near Rouen, where the fictional Dr. Bovary,
called to set a broken leg, first met and later
married Emma Rouault. Left: Dr. Charles and his patient,
M. Rouault (Richard Beale), Emma's father.

passionately with Mark Twain that "the difference between the right word and the nearly right word is the difference between lightning and a lightning bug." No wonder, then, that he brooded for a year and worked for four more years on *Madame Bovary,* by the measure of the day a short novel.

It is a very simple and melancholy story and its theme is the miserable ecstasy of infatuation. The wife of a sweet, dull country doctor tires of him and their provincial daily round, and after a glimpse of high life at the ball of a neighboring marquis, she dreams of a luxurious life in "exotic lands" or, at the very least, in Paris. She feeds this fantasy with expensive clothes and knickknacks from a rapacious haberdasher, whose bills will sooner or later have to be paid. She is attracted to a young neighbor, the apprentice to a notary, and is ripe for seduction. But she is not seduced. She smothers her impulse in an orgy of domesticity, retrieving her baby from its wet nurse but finding the baby as ugly as her husband. The young man, frightened off by what he feels for her and what he senses she feels for him, retreats to Paris.

After a less than sympathetic interview with the local priest, a man of massive insensibility, she meets a handsome bachelor squire and he overwhelms her. They fall into a love affair, all the more desperate for its stealth. Soon, the

From left: Francesca Annis as Emma; dalliance at
the piano as Emma and the young law clerk, Leon Dupuis (Brian
Stirner), are drawn to each other; a 19th-century
illustrator's vision of Madame Bovary.

squire tires of her, sends her a farewell letter, and she is insane with despair. She takes to the church again and seems cured and cowed, until the young notary returns on a visit, a more worldly and confident man than the youth she had resisted. She means to resist him again and writes him a cool letter of renunciation. But they are soon in a stew of passion from which, in time, they both recoil "like people who can stand only a certain amount of music . . . she was as sick of him as he was weary of her. Emma found again in adultery all the platitudes of marriage." Her end is swift. Badgered by her local creditors, in whom Flaubert invests all his detestation of the bourgeois provincials he lived among, Emma sees her husband go bankrupt, and her house and its belongings attached. She poisons herself with arsenic. The doctor dies in a stupor of grief.

The book came out, as did most novels in England and France, in serial parts. As soon as the last installment appeared, the government brought charges. The prosecution took its cue from the critics and maintained that the novel gave a distorted and malicious account of provincial life and that in the whole story the only virtuous character was the husband, who was left at the end as a helpless victim of the vice around him. The defense, countering by saying that the characters were drawn with absolute fidelity to life as it was and not as it might be, made its telling point when it contended that Madame Bovary had been depicted at all times as a wretched adulteress doomed to punishment by her own hand. It was a legal version of Henry James's offhand opinion: "It's hardly what you'd call family reading, but then again the whole book would make an admirable Sunday school tract." On this ground, that Emma Bovary— like Dumas's Camille—had come to a bad end, Flaubert was acquitted. Only months later, Baudelaire was prosecuted and convicted of "depravity and obscenity" for *The Flowers of Evil.*

Flaubert was often questioned in later years about the identity of "the real" Madame Bovary. He protested that what he had written was "a work of pure imagination." But long after his death, we have had access to his letters. One set of them—with their avowals of passion, spurts of hate, and tortured recriminations—amply satisfy the suspicion that in Louise Colet, a well-known poet, he had known a good deal of Emma Bovary. Colet had been his mistress during the four years of the novel's composition. He left her, one year before it started publication, out of unbearable obsession with his work. "Your mania for sentences," his mother said, "has dried up your heart." It may have been a passing petulant thought, but when Louise Colet was asked for the cause of the rupture, she replied: "No one but Madame Bovary."

119

Emile Zola
Thérèse Raquin

Balzac wrote and lived on the assumption that he was a force of nature, an element like fire, the ocean, volcanic rock. Flaubert was the quintessential man of letters, a professional's professional. Zola was, by contrast, a theorist and, considered as a novelist, a curiously pedantic one: a man possessed by a theory that fiction can be manufactured on scientific principles in a laboratory.

Even as a boy he was a fanatical believer in inherited characteristics, claiming to find in his own behavior and his talents powerful strains of the soldier, the priest, and the engineer who had appeared in his father's family. And whereas Balzac was at times attracted by passing fads like mesmerism and phrenology, Zola became, and remained, fascinated by the contemporary obsession with science. It must be said that he was in eminent company. He was a young man during the mid-century explosion of scientific research, when science seemed to apply outside its natural habitats of mechanics, chemistry, medicine. While it was exhilarating to hear of a Russian inventing electro-typing, an American vulcanizing rubber, the Swiss putting out electric clocks, and steamships racing across the Atlantic with the marvelous new screw propeller, it was thrilling to Zola to hear of the magic being taken out of the weather by meteorology, a Frenchman enunciating *Mathematical Principles Applied to the Theory of Wealth*, and Darwin delving into the holy of holies, the creation of Man, and coming up

Above: Zola by Nadar. Opposite: Scenes from "Thérèse Raquin," the story of a relationship inspired and destroyed by passion, and a vivid example of Zola's naturalism. Right: Thérèse (Kate Nelligan). Left: As she watches, horrified, her lover (Brian Cox) murders her husband (Kenneth Cranham).

with a scientific theory that rocked the world. (*The Origin of Species* was published seven years before *Thérèse Raquin*.) These wonders led many serious people to believe that science, far from being a special province of intellectual curiosity, was the thing itself—a method of inquiry that could be applied not only to industry and transport and surgery but to economics and religion. Why not to literature? So, Zola, in his twenties, while he was writing his first short stories, pretended to work out a "scientific" method of writing fiction. *Thérèse Raquin* was supposed to be the first demonstration of it. The critics were not impressed. They perversely looked on him as a literary man, and a pornographer at that.

Emile Zola was born in Paris in 1840 of a French mother and an Italian immigrant father who had made a name for himself as a civil engineer when he suddenly died. Zola, an only child, was left to a penny-pinching boyhood with a mother for whom his feelings were so mixed that during melancholy stretches he thought of himself as an orphan, which has been taken to explain why a number of his main characters—like Thérèse—are orphans.

He finished his schooling by failing to graduate and spent two years close to penury in a Paris slum. Just before his twentieth birthday he went to work as a salesman in a publishing house and remained there until he published an autobiographical novel—*Claude's Confession*—gamy enough to invite the threat of police action. But on the understanding that he would quit the publishing house, no charges were pressed. He was not put off by this criticism. He was enlivened by it. After all, Flaubert had been prosecuted for *Madame Bovary.* He would go one better, and he would create a monstrous Madame Bovary and a lover, a couple "without intelligence or free will, drawn to each other by nothing but their physical nature. Thérèse and Laurent are human animals." It was to be, wrote Zola, "a surgical examination performed without sentiment or moral judgments."

Thérèse and her husband might have been variant cartoons for Madame and Dr. Bovary. The wife is torpid, the husband is weak and well-meaning, and the pet of his mother, with whom they live over her haberdashery. There soon appears an old school friend of the husband's, a rougher type but a virile one. His attraction for Thérèse is immediate, and within a day or two they are making violent love in secret. The secrecy becomes unbearable. One Sunday, on a river picnic, the lover drowns the husband. This act, or the distortions of it in frequent nightmares, freezes the lovers' passion. In private, they become testy and are haunted by the husband's likeness in the morgue. In public, they behave with calculated warmth so as to suggest to old Madame Raquin's social circle the idea of marriage. After a year of this masquerade, during which Thérèse denies her lover all sexual contact, they are married. They at once begin to share delusions of seeing the corpse of the husband on the marriage bed. From then on, their enforced intimacy and the presence of Madame Raquin only exacerbate their guilt. In an appalling final scene, and in front of the paralyzed and now speechless old woman, even their recriminations become intolerable. They commit suicide.

The reception of *Thérèse Raquin* was even less sympathetic than that for Zola's squalid autobiography. The critics, out of charity or boredom, ignored the novel as a scientific experiment and dealt instead with Zola's alternative theory that he was "advancing the realism of Balzac and Flaubert." But he was accused of regression, of having invented "a guttersnipe Madame Bovary." Zola retorted that they had made the mistake of judging his characters as individuals. He was not interested in individuals, only in types. *Thérèse* was a first attempt at "examining the human heart on the operating table." (Zola's defenses of his writing are packed with medical, and especially surgical, metaphors. They would have come more understandably from Flaubert, who spent much of his youth haunting hospitals, fascinated by his father's acquaintance with surgeons and anatomists. Flaubert knew much more about these things but talked less, and resisted arranging them in a theory of novel-writing.)

122

Zola was not deterred. He insisted that he was on to something quite new in the history of fiction: to see humans as colonies of types, small organisms swarming in families in the large organism of society, to be examined with clinical disinterestedness. Believing this, he conceived in the following two years an immense project on the model of Balzac's *Human Comedy:* a cycle of novels about the heyday and decline of a single family. He did it, in twenty novels and thirty-three years.

In his fifty-eighth year, he became known throughout Europe to millions who had scarcely heard of Zola the novelist. He defended the innocence of Captain Dreyfus in a newspaper broadside denouncing the general staff of the French army. His conviction for libel was overturned but before the second trial he fled to England and stayed with a man who, nine years before, had gone to prison for translating Zola into English. He came home to France when the Dreyfus case was re-opened and the general staff was safely on the defensive. Undoubtedly, he thought Dreyfus innocent but his original broadside was wildly rhetorical and self-regarding, a very unscientific brief for the defense. Later on, he luxuriated in his role as the champion of the oppressed, as in his youth he had cast himself as the heroic defender of the early Impressionist painters. Outside his great gifts, he was nothing if not an exhibitionist. All his life, controversy was his hobby.

123

A world-famous headline of 1898 was Zola's denunciation
of the French government for covering up evidence that the disgraced
Captain Dreyfus was innocent. His paper sold 300,000 copies.
The case was avidly followed by Parisians (sketch), but
even so it took years to free Dreyfuss from Devil's Island.

Feodor Dostoyevsky
The Gambler Crime and Punishment The Possessed

One of the most tedious hobbies of amateur literary critics is that of the locksmith: of reading the lives of novelists in order to search out the "originals" on which they based their inventions, and thus turn each body of fiction into a grand *roman à clef*. Obviously, there has never been a writer of fiction who did not call on his own experience. The best work of the best novelists is grounded in their familiarity with the material they transmute, more or less, into fiction. Some do it much more and some much less.

"Crime and Punishment" featured John Hurt as Raskolnikov, the wretched protagonist. Expelled from the university, in Moscow, living in poverty, he determines to escape from his vile situation by murdering an old woman moneylender with an axe.

The striking exceptions are fantasists like Scott and Charles Reade who transport themselves into other times and delight us with the shock of recognition that human nature was as credible and complex in a remote or alien society as in our own.

But it has to be said of Dostoyevsky that among writers of the first rank only Tolstoy so thoroughly digested into the whole body of his work not only the human elements of his own life—in Dostoyevsky the peasantry, the army, the murders, betrayals, the pawnbrokers, police inspectors, landladies, prostitutes, priests, students—but the sequence of his beliefs and disillusionments, from atheism, socialism, liberalism, the theory and practice of revolution, and, in the end, redemption through the Christian church. The reader of Dostoyevsky who knows none of this need not feel deprived. If he does, the fault lies in him, for Dostoyevsky is one of those writers whose imagination only enriches and intensifies the actuality of the experiences he is writing about. What the innocent reader may doubt is the savagery, the unrelieved melodrama, of the lives of Dostoyevsky's central characters. A sketch of his life may help to dispel the suspicion that Dostoyevsky is inventing anything he had not known and suffered at first hand.

Feodor Mikhailovich Dostoyevsky was born in Moscow, in 1821, the son of an army doctor, a Ukrainian, and a Moscow merchant's daughter who died when the boy was sixteen. He was entered in the army engineering college in St. Petersburg and spent three painful years there relieved by anesthetic doses of Goethe, Balzac, Shakespeare, and Dickens. From them, from Dickens most, and from the life of the people around him, he became acutely aware of city poverty and impressed by the stoicism of the peasants—an admiration that did not waver when his father was murdered on his estate by peasants who could no longer stand his brutality. Dostoyevsky resigned his army commission and wrote a first novel, *Poor Folks,* that was immediately acclaimed as a masterpiece by the leading Russian critic of the day. After four more novels, he met and was converted by a Utopian socialist. He renounced all claims on his father's estate and disposed of a lump-sum settlement in a night or two of gambling. For much of his life Dostoyevsky was a pathological gambler.

Fired by his new socialist beliefs, he started to write inflammatory pamphlets and print them on illegal presses. (He also started to suffer from convulsions, which were later diagnosed as epileptic.) He made a rousing public speech demanding the abolition of censorship and an end to serfdom, was arrested, sentenced to death, and reprieved as he lined up with other prisoners on

126

the execution ground. His sentence was commuted by the Emperor to four years at hard labor, to be followed by service in the army as a private. He went off in chains to Siberia, stayed his four years, went back in the army and entered into a marriage that turned into a seven-year disaster. His epilepsy became too much for the army and he was released. Now in his late thirties, he was back in St. Petersburg wearying of socialism and beginning to brood on a problem that obsessed him for the next seven years, through the writing of *Crime and Punishment*: the conflict between the free will of the individual and his submission to God, if there was one. "A tortured child of unbelief," he called himself, and wrote a novel, *The Life of a Great Sinner*, in the forlorn hope of exorcising the torture.

In his fortieth year he made his first journey abroad and wrote two bitter commentaries, one on the grimy face of London, the other on the vulgar face of Balzac's Paris, which he followed with a memoir of his life in prison. Never able to achieve even short periods of serenity, he went to live in Moscow during a particularly harrowing time. His unloved wife was dying, his mistress had to be maintained, and he got involved with a shady publisher who paid him 3,000 rubles on the condition that a new novel was to be delivered within eighteen months if his copyright and the royalties on all his past work were not to be forfeited. Dostoyevsky hired the star pupil of a shorthand school and in three weeks dictated to her the entire manuscript of *The Gambler*.

It is a short novel intended as a strong purge of his compulsive gambling habit: the memoir of an addict who ruins himself at the roulette table and impatiently awaits—along with most of the cast of characters—a prime cut from the inheritance of a rich old lady who is close to death. However, she rallies, appears in the resort town, tries her hand at roulette, wins, and becomes the darling of her hopeful heirs until she yields to one last spin of the wheel. Dostoyevsky had once written to his sister: "I know the secret of how not to lose, I really do know . . . it consists in keeping one's head the whole time." After *The Gambler*, he knew better, but not for long: "It's not the winning, it's the game." He celebrated his swift delivery of the manuscript by marrying the hired stenographer and going off on a two-year honeymoon during which he gambled away his rubles, most of his personal belongings, and his new wife's possessions.

But throughout these personal crises and distractions, he fretted continually about the battle between the existence of God and the power of free will. He had been struck in Siberia by the will power, the seeming self-sufficiency, of the murderers he had lived with. In short, *Crime and Punishment* had been

127

Top: Dostoyevsky, ca. 1870, and his summer home at
Staraya Russa. Middle: Raskolnikov hears the lament of the
drunken Marmeladov (Frank Middlemass).
Bottom: Grandmamma (Edith Evans)
bucks the roulette wheel in "The Gambler."

brewing in him. He sat down to write it when his brother had died and left his sister-in-law impoverished, and when he himself was hounded by moneylenders, pawnbrokers, and police inspectors and alarmed by a general panic in the Russian economy. He set up the theme of the novel in a letter to his publisher:

It is to be a psychological account of a crime. The action is contemporary, this year [1865]. A young man—Raskolnikov—of petit-bourgeois background has been expelled from the university and is living in extreme poverty. Lacking seriousness and stability in his mental make-up, he has given himself over to certain strange ideas in the air at that time. He determines to escape from his vile situation at one stroke: to murder an old woman who lends him money for interest, and with that money to bring happiness to his mother (who lives in the provinces) . . . and to deliver his sister, a companion in a landowner's family, from the lascivious attentions of the head of the house.

No outline could be more succinct or so coolly suggest the tragic ironies with which Dostoyevsky would invest it. Of course, the murder brings happiness to no one but delivers Raskolnikov into the lion's den of an examining magistrate, his best friend's cousin. In the most masterly episodes of the novel, the magistrate becomes a friend of Raskolnikov's, indulges in philosophical fencing matches with him, tolerantly weighs the grain of truth that may lie in Raskolnikov's theory that ordinary men submit to the laws of the land whereas extraordinary men, like Napoleon, achieve a kind of integrity in imposing their own laws, by mass murder if need be. The magistrate tantalizingly describes the different techniques required to bring different types of murderer to heel. In the end, Raskolnikov's wits are no match for the magistrate's, but what leads him to surrender himself is the piety of a young prostitute who, with singsong sincerity, keeps impressing on him her simple belief that crime is sin and punishment is redemption. She goes off with him to Siberia.

In the light of this revelation, all the more compelling in having come from an artless, wholly unintellectual, girl, Dostoyevsky felt moved to re-trace the turmoil of his whole political history. It was time for this achingly honest man to attempt yet another self-administered purge. In his fiftieth year, he wrote *The Possessed*. It is about the mischief contrived in a provincial Russian town by a group of young and middle-aged revolutionaries whose leader has bound them to himself first by a vow of "dedication" and then, more firmly, by a threat to inform on anyone who leaks the knowledge of big and little crimes—blackmail, thievery, suicide—he has involved them in. It is admittedly the most autobiographical of Dostoyevsky's novels, an impassioned dramatization of the life of an ex-revolutionary grown to be outraged by the pettiness, the deceit, the

self-righteousness, the mistrust, and betrayals that he had come to believe are built in to revolutionary movements, successful or not. The dialogue spits with maxims bitterly learned: "All conspiracies must have presidents and first secretaries because they are [the work of] snobs"; and "The marks of a socialist are sentimentality and the fear of holding an opinion of his own."

In the end, Dostoyevsky went to the furthest extreme from his youthful socialism. He became a passionate conservative Christian who saw no worthy future for Russia except in "the body of Christ and a large, God-fearing peasantry" and no future for Europe unless it was united by Russia and the Orthodox Church. Conversely, he concluded that any attempt to force a master plan on society "can lead only to the end of the concept of God and to political bestiality." Ilya Ehrenburg said something about Dostoyevsky which is probably as frank as anything that dare be said aloud by a writer who hopes to survive in the Soviet regime: "Dostoyevsky told the whole truth about human nature, a truth which is undeniable but one which is deadly if one is to build a state." It is not surprising that after 1917 Dostoyevsky's view of truth was thought "too dangerous" to publish. However, his house in what is now Leningrad is respectfully laid out as a museum, but his books are as hard to find—in Russia—as ever.

"The Possessed": Tragedy overtakes a band of revolutionaries
when dedication to their cause leads to murder. Left:
Shatov (James Caffrey), the victim, with his sister Dasha (Anne
Stallybrass). Right: Verhovensky (David Collings), the
murderer, argues with distraught accomplice (Tim Preece).

Leo Tolstoy
Anna Karenina Resurrection

To sum up the life and work of Dostoyevsky in a few pages is brash enough but not so daunting as an attempt to do the same for Tolstoy, a genius as inventive as Balzac, a philosopher of history quite as serious as Carlyle, a religious convert very close in his torments and his ecstasies to the life of the saints, and a character of protean complexity. I can only hope to say a few useful things about the reflection of his life in two novels written at different times, when he was undergoing fundamental changes in his beliefs and his way of life.

One of the three central figures in *Anna Karenina* is the soldier, Vronsky, in his essentials the Tolstoy of early manhood, invented in a time of self-doubt during which Tolstoy was ready to renounce forever the life and the world he had grown up in. Count Leo Tolstoy was born, in 1828, a member of the old

*Married ten years, Anna Karenina leaves her proper
husband for a rakish officer, Count Vronsky–an adultery as
shocking as Emma Bovary's. Nicola Pagett (opposite) was Anna.
She and Vronsky (Stuart Wilson) are at the center of
the two rows in picture above. Left: Tolstoy at family estate.*

Russian landed gentry. His father, a count whose ancestor had been entitled by Peter the Great, married a princess who brought with her a substantial fortune. Both parents had died by the time the boy was eight, and he was thereafter brought up by adoring aunts, educated by French tutors, studied indifferently at the University of Kazan, and retired, as he thought, for life to his large country estate and the care of his serfs. But he was too restless for this pastoral life and—in a diary he kept from this time on—he confessed his ineptitude as an estate manager. He went to Moscow, frittered away a couple of years on

*Above: A distraught Anna, now carrying her lover's child, is
ill at ease with her husband Karenin, played here by Eric Porter.
Opposite: Vronsky has resigned his commission and
has retreated with Anna to a country estate, where they
live in adulterous exile.*

134

gambling and women, and then joined the army as a gentleman volunteer officer. He appears to have been a brave and competent soldier and fought in the Caucasus and in the Crimean War. After four years, he grew tired of the army too and rationalized his discontent in a series of published sketches that showed his superior officers unworthy of the simple soldiers they commanded.

After another bout of society life in St. Petersburg, he fell in with a literary crowd and learned to distrust their aesthetic theories and to detest the sententiousness of political progressives. He traveled widely in Europe in the flush of its new industrial and material prosperity, he hated all of it, came back to experiment with the education of peasant children, and at the age of thirty-four married a girl of seventeen and returned to his estate and his origins. He stayed there for fifteen years, learned how to run his estate, fathered thirteen children, was as happy as he would ever be, wrote *War and Peace* and, in his late forties, *Anna Karenina*.

It is a searching review of his youth, and in its last part a penitential document. Anna, an impeccable young matron, is married to Karenin, a high-minded businessman. She meets Captain Vronsky, a handsome and fashionably

*"Resurrection": Prince Dimitri (Alan Dobie, center),
having seduced the prostitute Katerina as a young girl, now
strives to save her from prison in Siberia. When all
fails, he follows her, thereby finding atonement
and resurrection. Opposite: Anna and Karenin.*

dissolute soldier. He takes one look at her and that is the end of his philandering. The affair is seen at once as a breach of the upper-class code, which permits illicit love affairs discreetly conducted provided, as Vronsky's mother says, "they don't become serious and turn into drama." Anna finds herself pregnant and her husband sends their son away to avoid contamination by his degraded mother, who is now torn between her passion and her guilt. But once her child is safely delivered, she professes a new tenderness for her husband, and he claims to have discovered "the Christian joy of forgiveness." The reconciliation is short-lived. Anna and Vronsky arrange a farewell meeting, but the old virus flares up again. They desert everybody and escape to Italy, where they eventually grow listless with satisfaction and return to St. Petersburg in the hope that society will have allowed the wound to heal. But society will have none of them. They must retreat again to the country, and they stifle in boredom. Anna takes to drugs, and Vronsky takes to increasingly frequent jaunts into the provinces on business and local politics. They have plumbed the depths of that nightmare holiday that seems to be the fate of unsuccessful adulterers. There is nothing for Anna to do but to go to the station where she had first met Vronsky and throw herself under a train.

The analogies with the life that Tolstoy had led are innumerable. And as a counterpoint to this main plot is the tale of two characters who represent the life that Tolstoy was then leading, from which he was hoping to emerge into a state of spiritual grace. Levin is a reformed rake who appears to enjoy a happy marriage among his tenants and the peasants he admires, with Jeffersonian fervor, as "the greatest of God's creatures." Punctuating this idyll from time to time is the appearance of his brother, a drunken radical who scorns this sentimental view of the land and "the people" and argues the case for Communism. And the tenor of Levin's marriage is ruffled at the start by his need to expiate a dissolute youth by insisting that his bride read a diary of his early peccadilloes. (A perilous bit of honesty in which Tolstoy himself had indulged and rued.)

The novel never settles into a single view of its characters or their situations. It oscillates, through Tolstoy's mercilessly honest observation of life, between the truth of a given moment and some permanent truth Tolstoy himself was battling his way toward: among the claims of society, even of its hypocrites; of the army and the discipline of duty; of the lovers' genuine devotion; of the hard, rewarding life of the peasantry; even of the germ of idealism in the Communist brother. The three hinges of the plot are Vronsky, the gallant lecher that

Tolstoy had been; Levin, through whom Tolstoy plagues himself with doubts about the secular joys of a prosperous landowner; and the husband, Karenin, who marks Tolstoy's own move away from a life of respectability to one of "Christian forgiveness."

Resurrection was written when he was seventy-one, at a time when he was riddled with guilt about the financial success of his writing, and had renounced the wealthy gentry, the duties of citizenship, all forms of political partisanship, and orthodox Christianity. It is a simpler story, partly because it is a polemical novel, partly because Tolstoy thought he had loaded *War and Peace* with too much "superfluous detail" and *Anna Karenina* with too much particularizing of a social world he had come to detest. It is the story of the struggle of a Russian prince to make amends for having seduced a girl of sixteen who subsequently became a prostitute. She is wrongly convicted of a crime and the prince devotes his life to an orgy of redemption, first taking up and losing her appeal, then making up to the beautiful wife of a high government official in the hope of securing a pardon from the Czar. When all fails, the prince and the girl go off together to Siberia. Although—like Dostoyevsky's Raskolnikov and his prostitute—they achieve a mutual redemption, the prince is shattered at last by the girl's refusal to marry him. To Tolstoy at that stage, a state of grace was not to be attained by any extreme of human love or sacrifice, short of resurrection through faith in Christ. In spite of the polemics, Tolstoy's idealism is everywhere mocked by his observation. And in spite of his late belief that literature should be written in the service of religion, he could not suppress the instinct that told him literature must reveal men and women as they are. What another writer would have rejoiced in—his unblinking sense of the rich disorder of life—drove him almost insane from the effort to discipline and arrange it into a noble harmony.

If there can ever be a last, best word on Tolstoy, I think that Isaiah Berlin has come closest to writing it:

Tolstoy's sense of reality was until the end too devastating to be compatible with any moral ideal which he was able to construct out of the fragments into which his intellect shivered the world, and he dedicated all of his vast strength of mind and will to the lifelong denial of this fact. At once insanely proud and filled with self-hatred, omniscient and doubting everything, cold and violently passionate, contemptuous and self-abasing, tormented and detached, surrounded by an adoring family, by devoted followers, by the admiration of the entire civilized world, and yet almost wholly isolated, he is the most tragic of the great writers, a desperate old man, beyond human aid, wandering, self-blinded at Colonus.

137

Arthur Schnitzler
Vienna 1900

The six playlets of this series were written by Arthur Schnitzler, who today seems hardly known to the young, and vaguely, and wrongly, remembered by the old as a light-fingered spinner of tales about Vienna in what we now choose to think of as the twilight of an imperial city. If so, it must have seemed to Schnitzler a very long and brilliant twilight. He was approaching sixty when the Austro-Hungarian Empire collapsed in the defeat of the Central Powers at the end of the First World War. For most of Schnitzler's life, Vienna was an industrial pioneer, a scientific and medical leader, and a cultural and musical capital unmatched in Europe.

Arthur Schnitzler was born in Vienna in 1862, the son of a Jewish doctor. He meant to follow in his father's footsteps, graduating from the school of medicine, practicing in and around various hospitals, and writing a lot of medical papers, significantly about the new specialties of hypnotism, psychology, and what Freud, who was first distinguished as a neurologist, began to call "neuroses." Not until he was nearing thirty did Schnitzler start to write stories

Arthur Schnitzler (above) gave up a medical practice in his mid-thirties to become a writer. He was a graceful stylist whose stories were fragile, but he saw people with clarity and compassion. Opposite: "Mother and Son"—Beate and Hugo Heinold (Dorothy Tutin and Christopher Guard).

and playlets. In his middle thirties, he quit medicine entirely and gave himself to literature.

He had two great vogues: the first around the turn of the century, when he was approaching his fortieth year; the second in the late 1920s, when he was close to seventy. He rode his first wave of popularity as a literary radical, something quite different from a radical writer. His protest, and his innovations, were against the prevailing forms of storytelling. He consciously dedicated himself to outdating the grinding naturalism and the pseudo-classicism of German fiction.

By the time of his second vogue, war and revolution had reduced Vienna to the capital of a small republic. And it would be logical to assume that

his reputation had succumbed with the empire. For by then, other radicals came along to date *his* school of fiction: men who used traditional literary forms to scorn the fragile substance of Schnitzler's stories, which were mostly about the irony or pathos of love affairs. Britain and America were blinking in the dust of a stampede of social realists: Shaw and Wells and Galsworthy, and Dreiser and Farrell and O'Neill, who either derided the structure of society or lamented the tragic loneliness of men *in* society.

How, then, could Schnitzler at such a time acquire a new and enviable reputation outside his own country, not least in the United States? I think the answer must be that when Vienna was in a social and political ferment, when the Social Democrats were running the city government, and when its workers' apartments were a new model for the world, many Europeans—Austrian conservatives most of all—rediscovered Schnitzler as a sheet-anchor of the old order

Left: Dr. Graesler (Robert Stephens) treats the ailing
daughter (Rebecca Saire) of Frau Sommer (Sheila Brennan)
an act that will change his status as "A Confirmed Bachelor."
Right: "Spring Sonata" brings lifelong penance to Berta
(Lynn Redgrave), left, and death to Anna (Jacqueline Pearce).

and, with him, distrusted "all state plans for the social mass known as the people." In America, where no social thunderstorms yet threatened the high noon of the Coolidge prosperity, Schnitzler offered an interesting, an exotic and deeper, variation on the romantic pathos of F. Scott Fitzgerald.

At any rate, society—as a political frame or a political enemy—was none of Schnitzler's business. He was deeply nonpolitical. He was interested, always had been, in particular people, and he was preoccupied with the relations between the sexes, both before and after, as Shakespeare put it, "the hey-day in the blood is tame." He once said flatly that "the main end of life is happiness." and that it can best be procured, however briefly, in the attraction of a man and a woman.

It was not much to go on when a quarter or more of the population was out of work, and in the Great Depression Schnitzler's reputation slumped again along with that of many larger talents. But his insight is keener than his surface material suggests. And we thought him worth reviving as an author whose grace of style disguises the depths of human behavior that he sensed in the most trivial happenings. I doubt that Freud would have been much taken with an author who was no more than a Viennese Michael Arlen, and Freud not only knew and admired Schnitzler as a friend. He said that Schnitzler's steady gift of probing beneath the surface of sexual relations had helped him greatly in his own psychoanalytical work.

For all the melancholy of his themes, Schnitzler was not, by all accounts, an unhappy man. When he died, his friends unearthed voluminous notebooks with the outlines of many stories about death. As a physician who had practiced for many years, he was, of course, well acquainted with death. It fascinated him, however, not as defeat, nor even release, but as a kind of wisdom that gave majesty to the meanest people. If he had known it, he would certainly have approved of Sir Walter Raleigh's apostrophe: "O eloquent, just and mighty Death! Whom none could advise, thou hast persuaded; what none hath dared thou hast done; and whom all the world hath flattered, thou only hast cast out of the world and despised: thou hast drawn together all the far-stretched greatness, all the pride, cruelty, and ambition of man, and covered it all over with these two narrow words, *Hic jacet.*"

As for Schnitzler's work among the living, it reflects in fiction the clinical conclusion of Freud's that the best psychoanalysis can do "is to help the patient bear the unhappiness that is common to mankind." It was Schnitzler's strength that he took this for granted. It was his charm that made it palatable.

141

Part 4

The Edwardians

Lillie

Any responsible biography of Edward the Seventh—Philip Magnus's or St. Aubyn's, for example—is bound to say a great deal about his steady interest in government and his enlightened view of Anglo-European relations but is likely to contain no more than two or three references to Lillie Langtry. (Andre Maurois's *The Edwardian Era* contains none.) By the time she appeared, when she was twenty-three and Edward was thirty-six, he had had a long string of mistresses, whom he enjoyed as adjuncts to a marriage that was remarkably happy and stable, thanks to Princess Alexandra's wise acceptance of "my husband's toys" and her evidently sincere belief that "jealousy is the bottom of all mischief and misfortune in this world." Lillie Langtry didn't last very long, but she was the Prince's first acknowledged mistress, the first to be publicly flaunted, at the races and in France, and her singular beauty and her willingness to exploit it as an early pin-up—by way of postcards, advertisements, and later a stage career—gave her a fame independent of her connection with the House of Saxe-Coburg-Gotha.

Unlike his grandson, Edward the Seventh did not drop a mistress and never see her again. He remained friends with most of his castoffs—the English ones, at any rate—and constantly demonstrated his kindly tolerance of women who had moved far out of the Marlborough House set, as witness his puzzled but continuous sympathy for Lady Warwick and her Socialist devotions.

And Lillie Langtry was one of those practiced exhibitionists who spin a web of scandalous rumors and hearsay about her person until the truth cannot be separated from the sheen of the legend. She lived on into the late 1920s, and her death rekindled the gossipy secrets of the Edwardians. Later, she became an obvious cameo subject for an American movie when someone recalled that during one of her American tours a Texas hamlet had renamed itself in her honor and begged her to visit the place. On a Western trip she held the train long enough to be presented with a six-shooter with which the late Judge Roy Bean had, in his whimsical way, maintained law and order west of the Pecos. And when, in the permissive 1970s, the fact could be finally disclosed, outside the royal family and its intimates, that she had borne a child by the father of Earl Mountbatten, a television drama about her was practically assured.

Like most of the great courtesans (and unlike Nell Gwynne, the Cockney sparrow who by good looks and sassy wits learned to sprout fine feathers in high society), her origins were modest and intensely respectable. She was born in 1853 on the largest of the Channel Islands, the daughter of the Anglican Dean of Jersey, one of those impeccable English clerics of upper-class education and scant middle-class means. Christened Emilie Charlotte Le Breton (Jersey has

Lillie Langtry, an actress of no great distinction,
was a beauty of renown whose liaisons made her a transatlantic
scandal and a darling of the public. Most famous of her
"lovers" was Prince Bertie, later King Edward VII. They were
played (opposite) by Francesca Annis and Denis Lill.

ancient bloodlines with Brittany and is, or was then, bilingual), she hated her given names and was called Lillie from girlhood on. She was the only girl among six brothers, and in the familiar way of a lone daughter scuffling with a household of callow males, she adopted the defense of being the local tomboy. But she had the advantage of her brothers' tutors and kept up with them in the classics, mathematics, French, German, music, and drawing. She was also nubile enough to receive a proposal of marriage from a young army lieutenant (the son of the Archbishop of Canterbury, no less) who, staggered to hear that she was only fifteen, applied for an immediate transfer and vanished from her story. She grew restless with the island life and found release from it in an apparently wealthy widower, one Edward Langtry, the possessor of several spanking yachts. She fell in love with *them* and married him. It was a debacle from the start. He was a moody drunk who lived far beyond his means, and the opulence—and the threatened scandal—that attached to her love affair with the Prince of Wales obliged her to maintain him for many years.

The only decisive part Langtry played in her life was to take her to London, where from the base of a London flat and with the help of an aristocratic Jersey friend, a patroness of the arts, she finagled her way into upper Bohemian society. Oscar Wilde became her friend. Burne-Jones painted her portrait. Her likeness was drawn and marketed as a popular miniature. She flitted upward into a circle of socialite peers and the visiting sprigs of foreign nobility, who descended on her like sailors on shore leave. Still in her early twenties, she had acquired enough tactical poise to be able to take her pick of these goatish patricians and once said, after rebuffing the King of the Belgians, "If I'm to be raped, I prefer to say who'll do it."

If she had been a Parisienne, she would have been known as a "grand horizontal." But in the blander aristocracy of Britain, she was accepted (not, of course, by Queen Victoria but "kindly and graciously" by Princess Alexandra) as "a dear friend" of the Prince of Wales, and subsequently of two other princes, a baron, various peers, writers, actors, and well-heeled misters.

The only person of more than frivolous interest in this catalogue of lovers is Prince Louis of Battenberg, the nephew of Edward the Seventh. Like all the royals of his day, he was intended for a princess, but when Lillie became pregnant with his daughter, he was eager to marry her. Edward, who never confused the claims of his mistresses with the claims of his heritage, absolutely forbade it, arranged for a discreet lying-in in Paris, and dispatched Battenberg to service at sea. Nothing, Edward insisted, must prejudice his nephew's naval

Top: Lillie captivates her prince. When they met in
1876, he was 36 and had just sat for the formal photograph
above. She was 23 and fetching, as is abundantly
clear from the drawing by a minor artist, Frank Miles, that
was widely sold as a "penny portrait."

146

*As an early "professional beauty" Lillie was chosen to
advertise Pears' Soap. (Actress Annis also posed as Lillie in
the legendary ad.) Her New York stage debut was reviewed by
good friend Oscar Wilde (Peter Egan). Above and opposite:
The extravagant social scene Lillie longed to join—and did.*

148

*Although her London performance as Cleopatra was acclaimed,
Lillie was essentially a theatrical curiosity. She was, however,
financially cushioned against the loss of her youth and beauty.
Above, Francesca Annis as Lillie in the role of Cleopatra;
opposite, the real Lillie in a photo by Nadar.*

career. It turned out to be a distinguished one. Some thirty-odd years later, Battenberg became the First Sea Lord (the navy's commander-in chief) and, without instruction, he mobilized the British fleet on the eve of the First World War. But his German name was his undoing. On the outbreak of war, there was a malevolent press campaign against him, and not even the private intervention of George the Fifth could repair its damage. Battenberg resigned and took the name of Mountbatten, as did his son (Lord Louis) and his grandson, Prince Philip, when he became a British subject and, in 1947, married Queen Elizabeth the Second.

The decline of Lillie into a mockery of her legend was slow but continuous. She took to the stage while her beauty was still ripe and became, on both sides of the Atlantic, more of a theatrical curiosity than an actress. In time, like most beautiful women who live by their beauty and the distinguished escorts who are fetched by it, she wound up without the beauty and with increasingly undistinguished escorts. However, she cushioned the afflictions of old age with substantial property holdings in several American states. In her late forties, she married "a tall, handsome, and ineffectual" baronet and was in old age content to have him, in between chorus girls, at home on the Riviera, where she died in 1929.

Yet, in her prime, she was a superior model of her type. George Bernard Shaw, surely no respecter of the social world she decorated, wrote of her: "I resent Mrs. Langtry. She has no right to be intelligent, daring and independent as well as lovely. It is a frightening combination of attributes." It was, anyway, a combination that threw into soft focus for a while the harsh glitter and rapacity of the society she enjoyed. The Edwardian age, like that of America's Gay Nineties, has passed into the popular imagination, and the media that cater to it, as an era of unabashed social splendor and unashamed romance and gaiety. No one has more rudely punctured this myth than Harold Nicolson, who, as a diplomat and the son of a diplomat, and a man married into an aristocratic family, saw Edwardian society from the inside:

The Edwardian age will, we may presume, live in history as an age of comfort. It was not. It was an age of fevered luxury; at the same time it was an age of peculiar human ineptitude. People possessed false values . . . . I do not regret that I was old enough to touch the fringe of Edwardian luxury. But I render thanks to Providence that I was also young enough to relish and share the wider liberties of our subsequent age. Let us be frank about it. The Edwardians were vulgar to a degree. They lacked style. They possessed only the hard glitter of their own electric light. . . . They lacked simplicity, and their intricacies were expensive but futile. . . . Nor, when all is said and done, can one forgive the Edwardians for their fundamental illusion. For it never dawned upon them that intelligence was of any value.

This son of a village schoolmaster, who grew up in a shoemaker's shop, and whose boyish games were played in the street of a Welsh hamlet remote from all the refinements of civilization and all the clangors of industrialism, announced to a breathless Europe without any pomposity of phrase, and with but a brief and contemptuous gesture of dismissal, the passing away from the world's stage of the Hapsburgs and Hohenzollerns. —HAROLD BEGBIE, 1921

151

Sixty years ago, no knowledgeable European or American, for that matter no Arab or Turk or Japanese, would have paused to guess the identity of this dazzling and cocky little figure who pronounced the doom of two empires. He was, he could have been, nobody but David Lloyd George, the presiding genius of British political history in the first quarter of this century, as Winston Churchill was in the second. Certainly, Lloyd George was the commanding civilian of the First World War as Churchill was of the Second. He had the same bristling energy, the same gift of inspiring morale, the same skill in mobilizing labor, industry, the politicians, and the mass of the people, and a more ruthless habit of forcing unpalatable tactics on the navy and the army chiefs. It is already a point of debate in Britain who is the greater figure. For, as the great wars have come and gone, Churchill's reputation is fixed in the conduct of them. But as more and more nations move inevitably—either by force or choice—toward the welfare state, Lloyd George comes into clear focus as the father of it. Nearly thirty years before Franklin Roosevelt, he was a radical liberal

Center: Chancellor of the Exchequer Lloyd George (Anthony Hopkins) confers with King Edward VII (Thorley Walters) about crisis brought on by House of Lord's unprecedented veto of his liberal "People's Budget." Left and right: Lloyd George and Hopkins in role.

who proclaimed a new deal for the poor and the middle classes in the teeth of a privileged opposition far more powerfully entrenched than Wall Street: against the House of Lords, the great landowners, the City financiers, the Church of England, and the factory owners. In his great years, in the decade before the First War, with his blazing eloquence and his almost clairvoyant intuition for sensing what most people hardly knew they wanted, he was not being too rhetorical in saying that he fought "for the nine-tenths of mankind who throughout recorded history have ground corn for the other tenth."

He is, in retrospect, one of those magnetic figures who await only a first-rate play to galvanize first-rate actors into wanting to play him. In our television play, Keith Dewhurst's cunning portrait was brought brilliantly to life by Anthony Hopkins, who contrived a smooth amalgam of the metal of Lloyd George's character with everything that was mercurial about it: the charm, the darting shrewdness, the fleeting affections, the wit, passion, disloyalty—all scored for his beguiling tenor. He became, and in a brief ninety minutes, what an Edwardian lady, who knew Lloyd George well, said of him: "He is clever and he is stupid; truthful and untruthful; pure and impure; good and wicked; wonderful and commonplace: in a word, he is everything."

He was born in 1863, the son of a Welsh elementary schoolmaster who died the following year, leaving his widow in poverty and his sons' upbringing in the hands of his bachelor brother, a humble shoemaker in a Caernarvonshire village of Methodist Celts, dominated in all directions by Anglican Tory landowners. The four of them made do in a cottage with the barest amenities. The shoemaker's savings amounted to sixpence a week. And it was this petty inheritance that made it possible for David, leaving school at the usual age of fourteen, to dream over the nighttime candlelight of the grandeur of a career as a local solicitor. We can get a grim hint of the underdog life of the people he was to represent from his first successful plea: to have Nonconformists buried in the parish churchyard. He leaped around the countryside preaching against the Tories and taking up the cases of every dispossessed Methodist, although he was already a lapsed believer and a hopping lecher whose wife, learning early, stood by him when he narrowly survived a paternity suit. Throughout his life, he found women irresistible, and they him. It is a fact we can write about casually today. In his day, Lloyd George was protected by the now-vanished tradition of press restraint.

In his twenty-seventh year, he barely defeated the local squire for a seat in Parliament (which he subsequently held for fifty-four years) and from

Lloyd George in 1911 with a young Liberal ally,
Winston Churchill. They were much alike: bristling with
energy, optimism, wit, and courage, and epitomizing
the indomitable spirit that brought Britain victory in two
world wars. Lloyd George also initiated social gains.

then on he never looked back. His bounding energy, his Celtic gift of the gab, his murderous wit, were devoted to withering comparisons between the City, the Church, the landowning establishment, and the deprivations of the people who had bred him. Only once did he put his political career on the line, when—against the jingoism of all classes but in accord with the sympathies of the Welsh Nationalists—he denounced the Boer War as an outrage and very nearly split his party.

In the Liberal landslide of 1906, he became a Cabinet minister for the first time, and for the next five or six years, most effectively as Chancellor of the Exchequer, he terrified the Tories as Roosevelt was to petrify the Republicans. He closed the workhouses, he gave the merchant seamen their first decent wage, he introduced old-age pensions. He proposed to a responsive House of Commons to institute unemployment insurance and set up a national system of labor exchanges. He even expounded on the blessings that would flow from a national health-insurance system. But who, asked the appalled House of Lords, was to pay for these no-doubt humane reforms. "You, my Lords," was the short answer. The long answer was given in a "People's Budget," which would tax unearned income on land and land sales, stiffen death duties, and impose the first supertax on the rich. The House of Lords, which constitutionally kept its hands off the budget, sparked a constitutional crisis by rejecting it, and the issue went to a general election. Lloyd George bustled around the cities spouting his impish oratory ("A fully equipped Duke costs as much to keep up as two dreadnoughts") and was loyally echoed by his equally eloquent Liberal lieutenant, Winston Churchill ("This second chamber as it is—one-sided, hereditary, unpurged, unrepresentative, irresponsible, absentee"). In a new Liberal government, the budget passed the House of Commons. Within two years, an act of Parliament abolishing the veto power of the Lords led to its later emasculation, so that today it is an impotent but useful debating society conducted by men and women, many appointed for life only, who have no power to gain and no seats to lose.

In 1911, a year that to British Tories and American Republicans may become "a date which will live in infamy," Lloyd George crushed or seduced or placated the opposition and put through Parliament the first national health-insurance act. It was then, and not in the Roosevelt New Deal or in the inflationary surge of the 1960s' Great Society, that the welfare state was born. Which now, in Britain and America, is seen either as an unending flight into huge government expenses that must be arrested, or an historic move into a humane society that must not be reversed.

Mr. Rolls and Mr. Royce

The Big Business epic has not been a standard Hollywood product, very likely because the sound film did not get really under way until the 1930s, when the Depression fell on big business like the curse of a wrathful god, and Franklin Roosevelt appeared as a Daniel come to judgment.

Yet it is only since the Depression that successful examples of the form have been made, and the reason is not hard to seek. They are all rooted in nostalgia for the dear dead days—eons away from research and development teams and cost-effective analysis—when one humble ingenious Yankee tinkered in a shed and produced, to the initial scorn of the bankers (the very people who had let us down, were they not?) the rude prototype of what would soon emerge as a technological miracle and a boon to the common man. Mickey Rooney as young Tom Edison, Don Ameche as Alexander Graham Bell are the archetypes. (Odd that Henry Ford still awaits his movie citation.) It is an interesting point that Europe—where the banker and the captain of industry have never been conspicuous folk heroes, or villains—should have left to Hollywood the sanctification of Julius Reuter and the House of Rothschild.

It is even more remarkable that movie producers, riffling through the records of genuine Horatio Algers on this side of the Atlantic and the British exemplars of Samuel Smiles's *Self-Help* on the other, should not have stumbled with squeals of gratitude on the marvelous story of Henry Royce. The BBC's ninety-minute version was, if anything, unduly restrained in recounting the rags-to-riches facts of this remarkable life. Understandably, since a year-by-year recital of Royce's penury, his hopes and setbacks, would have made the drama as lugubrious, and comical, as a Victorian ballad.

Henry Royce was born, in 1859, in a Lincolnshire village, one of five children of a failing miller. He eked out the family living by scaring crows for farmers. When his father went broke and took two of his children to London, Henry was eight with one year of elementary school behind him and only one more year to come. He went to work on the streets as a newsboy and spent most of five years scrounging unsuccessfully for a steady job. He lived on one meal a day of bread and milk. But when he was fourteen, he received the windfall of a promise from an aunt to pay for his apprenticeship in a railroad repair shop. For three years he learned how locomotives worked and picked up a knack for making the most of hand tools. However, in the depression of 1880, his aunt couldn't keep up his apprentice's payments and he was let go. He went looking for a job on the road and walked to the North, sleeping in fields and flophouses. Ninety

156

miles north from where he had started, he found work in a Leeds munitions factory, and at nobody's bidding used the spare time from a fifty-four-hour week to jigger with electricity. Since he knew no mathematics or any other speciality that could be learned from books, he proceeded—as he was to do throughout his life—on a grinding trial and error system. Electricity excited him more than armaments, and he gave over his nights to classes at a technical college. He answered a newspaper advertisement and to his delight was accepted as a "tester" in the thrilling new enterprise of the London Electric Light and Power Company, where he astonished the management with his manual skill and was appointed, at nineteen, the electrical engineer in charge of converting the street lighting of the city of Liverpool to electricity. Surely this was the first rung on the ladder. So it was, but not on the ladder of advancement with this firm, which—a victim of the city fathers' fear of this perilous invention—went bankrupt and left Royce again on his own.

"Rolls-Royce": This famous partnership linked a wealthy,
Eton-Cambridge sportsman, Charles Stewart Rolls (left),
and an impoverished, self-taught mechanical genius, Frederick
Henry Royce. Opposite: Vintage car (used in series) is six-
cylinder, 40/50 h.p. Silver Ghost of 1907.

North again, to Manchester, where he had the luck to make a friend of a man who possessed the enormous sum of fifty pounds. Royce's monkish needs and his habit of thrift had rewarded him with twenty pounds in savings. The two pooled their fortunes and formed a company to manufacture filaments, electric bells, and dynamos. It prospered for the next ten years, during which Royce's fame as an almost hysterically perfectionist mechanic spread through the business, and his notoriety as a driving employer became a byword.

In 1894, in a move that foreshadowed his mastery of the automobile engine, Royce developed an incontestably engineered, indestructible electric crane as a superior alternative to the steam cranes then in use. However, his mulish obstinacy in persistently refining and testing every model, whatever the cost, lost him the market to cheaper American and German types. Still, he was established as a leading dynamo maker, and he was better than solvent. At the age of forty, in 1899—a very late date in the history of the automobile—he bought one. It was a French Decauville. Characteristically, he was dissatisfied with it, as he was with every other car he examined. Whereas the growing army of automobile buffs marveled at a contraption that could whiz along at fifteen or twenty miles an hour, Royce noticed only the noise and the chattering vibration. He resented the vibration and abominated the noise. He decided that the only tolerable automobile would be one he built himself. Throughout the days and nights of one whole winter (1903–4), he and two apprentices knew no other life than the building of the first Royce car. Some nights, Royce slept on the factory floor, other nights he slumped over the radiator. It was finished in February, and within the month a shareholder in Royce's company wrote a letter to a rich London friend, an automobile salesman, suggesting that this ten-horsepower, two-cylinder original might be worth inspecting. The recipient of the letter was the Hon. Charles Rolls, twenty-seven years old and the son of a peer.

Of the pair that was to hyphenate into the most distinguished car manufacturer on earth, Rolls is, in one way, the more freakish of the two. In only one way, but it was the one eccentricity that could forge the link between these two vastly different men born at the opposite ends of the social scale. In a word, young Rolls was the only Etonian on record who ever kept a dynamo in school, a hobby which was not only bizarre but, in a system of classical education that tended to hold an engineering degree in well-bred disdain, was a joke or an embarrassment to his schoolmasters. He went on to get that degree— in mechanical engineering—at Cambridge, but in everything else, his upbringing, his politics, his hobbies, his outlook, Rolls was a familiar type of the wealthy, upper-class, unscholarly youth, destined for Eton and Trinity, given to

159

*Top: Michael Jayston as Royce and Robert Powell as Rolls
with their first production car, the two-cylinder, 10 h.p.
model of 1904. Right: Rolls in Silver Ghost. Above: The
unlikely partners discuss plans. Royce carried on after Rolls
died in 1910 in the crash of an early airplane.*

mechanical toys when young and to fast cars in college. After Cambridge, Rolls decided on the peculiar career of an automobile enthusiast. He traveled through France and Germany examining cars, as another man might taste wines, and in 1902 he set up shop as an automobile repairer and salesman. He, too, was unhappy with the foreign models he sold, though they were superior to the English product. He, too, was dissatisfied with the imperfections of these early models—the noise especially—but as a mere aficionado, he had to assume that they were inherent in the invention itself. In Royce, he discovered to his joy, he had met the man who could set them right.

Nine months after their first meeting, Royce took on a back-breaking commission: he would make and deliver for Rolls four separate types of car, from a ten horsepower with two cylinders to a thirty horsepower with six cylinders, in all, ninety-nine actual cars. They were delivered. They were to be known as Rolls-Royces. They won golden prizes at shows in Paris, and at the races in the Isle of Man and between London and Monte Carlo. In 1906, the two men merged and founded the company that bears their names.

That is, for our purpose, practically the end of the story. Royce created the machine, and Rolls created the market—of the fussy, the rich, the rising plutocrat, the Indian princes, and the royal family. One year after the birth of the company, Rolls met Wilbur Wright, saw the airplane as the new wonder of the age, failed to interest Royce in an aircraft engine, and turned from the automobile to a passion for flying. In the spring of 1910, he resigned as managing director of the company and in the summer was killed in an airplane rally.

Royce went on designing and redesigning engines for cars, for tanks and airplanes in the First World War, and beyond. Before then, in 1911, his health failed and he was never again the steely, obsessive character of his first fifty-two years. But in public he made light of his afflictions, which didn't prevent him from urging teams of mechanics to take everything apart and instilling in everybody under him the fanatic principle that nothing is perfect which can be further perfected. He died, at seventy-five, in 1934.

So both of them were long gone before that shocker of a day, in February 1971, when Rolls-Royce—having planned the jet engine to surpass all jet engines, having gone beyond its first development estimate of 65 million pounds to 170 million, having involved the government in advances of 89 million and another 18 million in bank loans—was allowed to go bankrupt. Three weeks later, this paragon of free enterprise, built on a capital investment of 70 pounds, was reborn as a nationalized industry.

Shoulder to Shoulder

Shoulder to Shoulder was the story of the militant English suffragettes. The title is the first phrase in a marching song written expressly for them by a formidable proponent of the cause, Dr. (once the rebellion was over, Dame) Ethel Smyth who, in her day, was Britain's foremost woman composer. Her other compositions were far more ambitious. She wrote several operas, a Mass in D, many songs, and much chamber music. Like Sullivan's "Onward, Christian Soldiers," or Elgar's "Land of Hope and Glory," "Shoulder to Shoulder" is probably the work by which the composer would least wish to be remembered. But Dr. Smyth conducted it with a toothbrush from behind the bars of Pentonville prison, and as the battle cry of a doughty feminist it must stir her old bones in the grave.

Now that the suffragette movement has been reborn in Women's Liberation, it becomes a touchy matter to say who conceived it. For national pride is also quickened, and when, in the unpredictable course of time, the Russians latch onto it, no doubt we shall hear that a bourgeois intellectual born in Vladivostok anticipated Mrs. Emmeline Pankhurst by fifty years, just as—according to a categorical news release out of Moscow over twenty years ago—"beizbol" was declared to be a regulation Russian game before Abner Doubleday had ever been heard of. On second thought, it occurs to me that the Soviets could plausibly claim that their system has never required a feminist rebellion, since at least half their doctors are women and the ratio of female to male engineers is beyond anything the Western nations are likely to match until engineering becomes a compulsory first-year course in college.

At any rate, the genesis of feminism as a philosophical debating topic, if not yet a political movement, is to be found in a startling and eloquent tract, *A Vindication of the Rights of Women,* written as long ago as 1792 by Mary Wollstonecraft, whose daughter is far better remembered for marrying Shelley and creating Dr. Frankenstein and his ghoulish monster. But for nearly eighty years after its first stormy reception, the *Vindication* was regarded as a virtuoso rhetorical exercise. Not until 1869 did John Stuart Mill move onto the barricades with a blistering invective piece, *On the Subjection of Women,* which left the male establishment rattled but unshaken. Incidentally, in the same year, two American women—Miss Susan B. Anthony and Mrs. Elizabeth Cady Stanton—decided to renew the call for women's suffrage, which Miss Stanton and Lucretia Mott had first sounded at a women's convention in Seneca Falls, New York, in 1848. Anthony and Stanton formed a close friendship and cemented it for life in the National Women's Suffrage Association. It is impossible to overrate their achieve-

*Mrs. Emmeline Pankhurst (Sian Phillips), prime mover of the
suffragette campaign, with daughters Adela (Louise Plank),
left, Christabel (Patricia Quinn) and Sylvia (Angela Down),
right. Postcard: The sisters as children. Opposite: Annie
Kenney (Georgia Brown) cheers as Emmeline gets out of jail.*

ment for sheer persistence in a losing cause. They began dramatically enough by calling a convention to claim for women the voting rights granted to Negro men under the Fifteenth Amendment after the Civil War. Their crusading impulse never waned, but decade after decade its social effects were negligible. These two tenacious warriors appeared at annual suffrage conventions for fifty years. Time and again they were reluctantly permitted to testify before committees of Congress that were sometimes contemptuous and always unsympathetic.

The American testimony was inevitably well known to women members of the British intelligentsia, but Susan Anthony and Elizabeth Stanton had been battling away for twenty-nine years before the appearance of their British counterparts who, within six or seven years, emerged out of genteel discussion groups and a literature of protest into a national scandal and an effective one.

The practical pioneer of the cause was a male, one Richard Pankhurst, an upper-middle-class lawyer living in Manchester, the Northern seedbed of much other social protest: the Chartist riots, the Anti-Corn Law League, the Free Trade movement. He was a friend of John Stuart Mill and, indeed, had drafted the first women's suffrage bill, which died in the House of Commons in 1870. Nine years later, he married Emmeline Goulden, the daughter of a prosperous calico printer who shared his concern for the gross discrimination against women built into the law. For several years, they could do little but encourage discussion of these inequities, but they in turn indoctrinated their daughters,

Above: Mrs. Pankhurst and her counterpart in "Shoulder to Shoulder," Sian Phillips. Opposite: The real Annie Kenney, a North Country mill hand and an eloquent speaker, was one of the few working-class women to join the movement. Most of them were educated and well-to-do gentlewomen.

Christabel and Sylvia. Pankhurst's sudden death, in 1898, was the spur to the widow's resolve to convert his concern into a crusade. In 1903, she founded something called the Women's Social and Political Union. Building on a nucleus of friends, they recruited the like-minded in and around Manchester: still mostly upper-middle-class professional people. They printed broadsides, held rallies and harried politicians, but attracted few influential allies, except for one old Scotch Socialist, Keir Hardie. To the newspaper cartoonists they offered a new and hilarious target. From the working classes they received derision, and from every-

165

THE CAT AND MOUSE ACT

PASSED BY THE LIBERAL GOVERNMENT

THE LIBERAL CAT
ELECTORS VOTE AGAINST HIM!
KEEP THE LIBERAL OUT!

BUY AND READ "THE SUFFRAGETTE" 1d

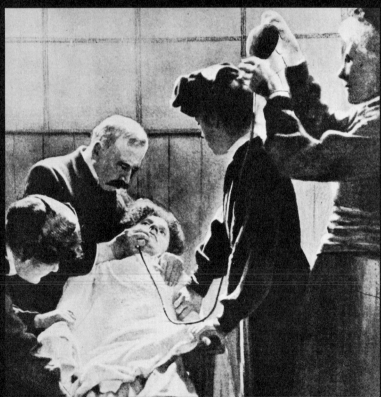

*Although suffragettes courted arrest (top) with their
violent protests, they won sympathy when the government harshly
forced-fed jailed hunger strikers (above and opposite).
Election poster hits Liberals for cat-and-mouse release and
re-arrest of forced-feeding victims.*

TORTURING WOMEN IN PRISON

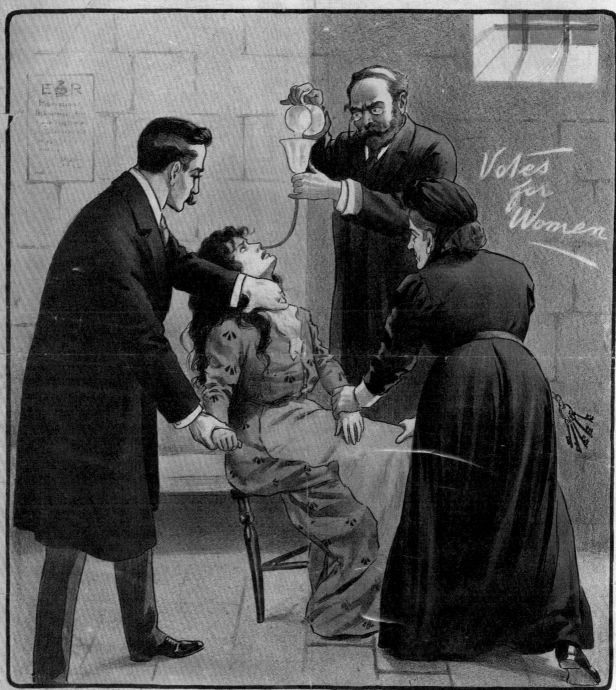

PUBLISHED BY THE NATIONAL WOMEN'S SOCIAL AND POLITICAL UNION   4 CLEMENTS INN STRAND W.C.   & PRINTED BY DAVID ALLEN & SONS LD 180 FLEET ST E.C.

VOTE AGAINST THE GOVERNMENT

body else indifference. Painfully, they made the political discovery that nothing is stronger in opposition than the power of apathy. So they made what turned out to be an historic decision: they decided to become a nuisance. They heckled and disrupted a Liberal-party election rally in Manchester led by the incoming Foreign Secretary, Sir Edward Grey, and a Conservative renegade, the new radical Liberal, Winston Churchill. To their great satisfaction, the Pankhursts saw the odium of their cause publicized and deplored in the national press.

The effect of their tenacity and courage, in the face of general ridicule, was to bring into their movement other idealists from outside their limited social circle: a young noblewoman, Lady Constance Lytton, who had previously had no other interest in what we call "the people" than an artsy-craftsy enthusiasm for folk dancing; the wives of other lawyers; one or two skeptical union organizers; the despairing wives of chronic alcoholics; and, most effectively, a North Country mill worker, one Annie Kenny, who pierced the pervading atmosphere of indignant gentility with the energy and earthy eloquence of a convinced working woman. She and the Pankhursts received a handsome subsidy from a wealthy couple, the Pethick-Lawrences, and they decided the time was ripe for an invasion of London.

The time was 1907. The decision was to forswear their failing tactics of appeals and protests to Parliament and to embark on a campaign of militancy. They organized roving bands of suffragettes—hardly credible yet as anarchists in their ladylike ensembles, their veils and gloves—who stuffed fire bombs in mailboxes, started fires, broke the windows of fashionable men's clubs and fought the oncoming police. The police retaliated first with prison sentences and then with the brutal and actually perilous tactic of forced-feeding of the hunger strikers.

When a new Liberal government under Herbert Asquith came in with an overwhelming mandate, the suffragettes took heart and paused to await the legislating of the women's vote. It did not happen. Asquith was a born temporizer and hairsplitter (both then and in his later reincarnation as a wartime Prime Minister). Also, as a man whose mother had been a humble weaver, he was execrated by the suffragettes as a traitor to his class. But the sheer din and ubiquity of their militant tactics paid off in the promise of a frightened government to draft a bill for female suffrage on the understanding that there would be an end to violence. There was a courteous pause between the death of Edward the Seventh and the crowning of George the Fifth. Asquith now introduced his bill, which turned out to be a mockery called the Manhood Bill, extending the

Mrs. Pankhurst being arrested outside Buckingham
Palace in 1914. The onset of World War I brought the movement
to a halt, as suffragettes joined the war effort. They got
the right to vote, partially in 1918, fully in 1928,
without fanfare—much earlier than most of Europe.

vote from men of property to all males, but not to women. Accordingly, the suffragettes went on a new and more systematic rampage of militancy during which all the leaders—including Mrs. Pankhurst—shuttled in and out of prison while the more independent daughter, Christabel, a sort of boutique Lenin, dictated the tactics of violence from voluntary exile in Paris. The government, holding on to its big stick, gingerly offered a carrot in the form of a bill (popularly known as the Cat and Mouse Bill) that acknowledged the growing abhorrence of forced-feeding. Wherever the practice was certified by a prison doctor to be a health hazard to an individual, the prisoner would be released.

After this betrayal, the militancy of the suffragettes became an irregular routine, like the later violence of the Irish Republican terrorists in London. It would spurt for a while, die down, erupt again, on into the summer of 1914, when Mrs. Pankhurst bowed before the fact that the turn of history is often called, not by the courage of reformers, or the rightness of their cause, but by some enormous accident on the outside. The First World War was that accident, and it gave daily proof that women everywhere on the home front, and in base hospitals as far apart as France and Mesopotamia (most of it today's Iraq), were at least the equals of men in work and courage and their superiors in endurance. In 1919, without the provocation of fire bombs, police brawls, or marches outside Parliament, women got the vote, but then only married women and female university graduates over the age of thirty. In 1928, the suffrage was extended at last to all women over twenty-one (as a lingering echo of male petulance, it was known as the Flapper's Vote).

As a footnote to the British experience, it is worth recalling that of the thirteen original colonies of this country, women enjoyed the right to vote in eleven of them until it lapsed under the discreet provision of the American Constitution to leave the dispensation up to each state. It then took 133 years, through the passage of the Nineteenth Amendment in 1920, for women to get the vote in every state of the Union. In most of the countries of the world, including Europe, they didn't get it until after the Second World War.

Mrs. Pankhurst said in old age that it took American women so much longer than the British to carry their cause because they refused to act by other than peaceable means. What was at the time improbable, but decisive, about the English pioneers was that they, of all nationalities, should have been the militants. Like many earlier and later advocates of populist causes, they discovered something that is the most baffling and terrifying political fact of our time: the success of violence.

170

She is a fine figure of a woman, superbly oblivious of those changes in the social order which agitate the more observant *grandes dames* of her period. When the war broke out she took down the signed photograph of the Kaiser and, with some solemnity, hung it in the men-servants' lavatory . . . [Her hotel] is a like a country house. She is a great one for sales, and whenever one of the great houses is being sold up, she takes away something for old times' sake. . . . It is the sort of house in which one expects to find croquet mallets in the bathroom . . . as a matter of fact, all you are likely to find in your room is an empty champagne bottle or two and a crumpled camisole. . . . Her parlor contains a comprehensive collection of signed photographs. Most of the male members of the royal families of Europe . . . young men on horses riding in steeplechases . . . elderly men in yachting caps. . . . There are very few writers or painters and no actors, for she is true to the sound old snobbery of pounds sterling.

Evelyn Waugh was describing the proprietress of his fictional hotel in *Vile Bodies* but he intended, and everybody knew, her as Rosa Lewis in her prime, the owner, hostess, and dictator of the Cavendish hotel on Jermyn Street, London. In his second television essay in Edwardian and Georgian manners, John Hawkesworth chose to call her Louisa Trotter and locate her establishment, the Bentinck, a block away from the Cavendish. But this dramatization (done by many of the same team that wrote *Upstairs, Downstairs*) was so close to the life of the original that to discuss the

The real Rosa Lewis (left) with Starr the doorman and
Fred the dog, who were fixtures for many years. Right: John
Cater as Starr, stand-in as Fred. Center: Gemma Jones
as Louisa and Christopher Cazenove as Charlie,
Lord Haslemere, father of her secret little daughter.

character and story line of her impersonation would only confuse the portrait of the outrageous reality.

Rosa Lewis, then, was born in a seedy part of London in 1869, the daughter of a clockmaker, a mouse of a man intimidated by a wife given over to hourly lamentations over the shame of having married beneath her. This dreadful mother and the gloom of her household were too much for Rosa, and at the age of twelve she left home and school and hired out as a "skivvy," the lowliest maid-of-all-work, to a shabby genteel family. After four years of this servitude, she moved slowly and painfully up the social scale of her employers until, in her late twenties, she contrived to enter a society household as an under-kitchen maid. Even in her teens she nourished what for a girl of her class was an absurd ambition: "To be the best cook in London." In time she was made responsible for buying the groceries, by no means a negligible chore in the eyes of the French chef. To him she dared to mention her wild ambition and her willfulness eventually won him over. In the first lesson, he laid down his first principles: begin with A, move on to B, and in time you might be permitted the privilege of attempting C. A represented "the nostrils," the importance of what you smelled. B was the purchasing of fresh raw materials. C was the art of cooking: to treat the materials "simply and with respect" (a lesson to us all). She was an untiring

173

Rosa Lewis (opposite), a soft-hearted Cockney autocrat,
and her remarkable hotel, both at the height of their fame.
The hotel was on Jermyn Street, south of Piccadilly,
served excellent food, offered unpredictable service, and had
its own horse-drawn carriage for guests and luggage.

and imaginative pupil and soon was allowed to cook for small but important dinners. Whether or not her autobiography is to be believed, the legend has by now hardened into fact that while the chef was on vacation in his native France, the household was thrown into panic by the Prince of Wales's acceptance of a forgotten invitation; that he came to dinner; that Rosa cooked the meal; that his Royal Highness was greatly impressed by it; and that he sent for her and pressed a gold coin in her hand with the line, "Here is a new sovereign from your future sovereign."

In later life, Rosa liked to drop guileful hints that she had indeed been the future king's mistress. Certainly, she had once been, if not a beauty, a handsome and formidably sensual woman. If she did go to bed with Edward, as Florence King has reflected, "It must have been a clamorous encounter."

At any rate, what is matter of fact is that she married a butler and set herself up in a substantial house with money mysteriously acquired, and then purchased a rundown hotel in St. James's. Out of its kitchen she catered dinners for fashionable people, but the husband, a shiftless man with an itch for the bottle, propelled the place into near bankruptcy. She ran him out of the house, she liked to say, "at the point of a carving knife."

At this low point—though she didn't know it—she was about to plant the seed of her lifelong prosperity. The preliminary groundwork was exhausting in the extreme. To pay off the appalling load of bills long overdue, she began to cater dinners for great houses (among them the Churchill's and the German embassy), doing all the buying and cooking for dinners for as few as four and as many as twenty-four persons. (Her record was twenty-four eight-course dinners in one week.) This ceaseless labor bought off the lease on the hotel, and by 1904 the Cavendish was launched on its prosperous and eccentric mission as an alternative London house and home for aristocrats, soldiers, polo players, bishops, teetering ladies from the Home Counties, American socialites, and such celebrities in transit as Charlie Chaplin, John Hay Whitney, and the Kaiser. Edward the Seventh had a permanent suite for incognito visits. One society girl said that the only people who had a sure passport to the Cavendish were "the three A's": the aristocrats, the Americans, and the affluent. She might have added—the impoverished sons of favorite clients killed in the First World War, officers on leave during the Second War, and pinched but likable rakes. For these she relieved their main embarrassment by transferring their accounts to the bills of departing guests who, for one offensive reason or another, she had not taken to.

175

Louisa Leyton (Gemma Jones) was the fictional version of London's finest French chef of the Edwardian era. She induced a master chef to teach her the art of haute cuisine, cooked a superb emergency banquet for the Prince of Wales, who rewarded her with "a new sovereign from your future sovereign."

By her own admission she was a terrific snob, but her snobbery was a peculiar code of her own devising whose originality fascinated and intimidated everybody. She loved a title, but no one could be more uncomfortable in the Cavendish than what we now call "the beautiful people," wandering fashion plates who are celebrated only for being celebrated. She was flattered by the well born but never mislaid a Cockney vowel nor picked up an aitch. She cherished eccentrics high and low. One of her favorites was Sir William Eden, a peppery Edwardian baronet (the father, by the way, of Anthony Eden) who wore purple waistcoats and hated perfume, Whistler, children, smoking, and dogs. When she decided on a whim to close the place for a month, he wrote: "Mrs. Lewis— Charming Woman: Good. When you re-open, will you please turn out that damned dog before I have to murder it, or you—you for choice——Yours in ever increasing affection, (Sir) William." Another favorite was a tense, penurious clergyman who was prized for his choice assortment of conversational starters,

The Elinor Glyn Room of the Cavendish honored the British author of several novels whose steamy eroticism made them both controversial and phenomenally popular. "Three Weeks," in particular, became grist for the Hollywood mill of the silent era. Rosa never minded controversy.

one of which went: "Curious thing, none of the males in my family ever grows his canine teeth."

Apart from the appeal of her unpredictable behavior, there were two other rarities that made the Cavendish a hotel unlike any other before or since. First, the cooking maintained, until the Second World War, the standards exacted of her by her teacher. Escoffier himself was an open admirer of a bill of fare that could offer, as a cold weekday dinner: "Consommé with chicken wings. Cold trout Cavendish. Whitebait. Soufflé of quails. Beef in aspic. Polish ham with *fèves* beans. Cold chicken Parisienne. Salad. Asparagus *en branches*. Poached peaches with chestnuts. Ice-cream mold. *Friandaises*. Oysters wrapped in bacon and pounded mushrooms."

The other enticement, to people of either respectable or philandering persuasions, was the original way in which the hotel was run. In the early 1900s, there were few hotels for upper-class people to stay in, and they were very formal. Respectable people dined at home. Rosa Lewis decided that there would be no public dining room, no keys to the rooms, no tips till the end of the stay, and no hotel register. You signed a guest book before you left, if you chose, and if she wanted you back. The hotel was divided into suites, each with its drawing room, dining room, bedroom, and bathroom. These arrangements were useful on several grounds. They offered privacy to retiring types, and to socialites on experimental assignations, a maximum of temptation with a minimum of publicity.

Mrs. Lewis did have her run-ins with the press, noticeably in the 1920s, when gossip columnists began to spawn. In 1925, the London *Daily Mail* carried a splashy story about an unauthorized biography of Rosa called *The Queen of Cooks—and Some Kings*. But on a threat of court action, the paper reluctantly invited Rosa to write a scalding repudiation of the book as a fraud and a travesty.

The heyday of the Cavendish was very long, but after the Second War the austerity of a still severely rationed country made those precious "fresh raw materials" hard to come by. Rosa lost her zeal for cooking. Rude social change stripped her of dependable help, and the old carefree clients were gone with their inheritances and their lordly habits. The place settled into a kind of memorial seediness, and the old lady sat in her big chair off the foyer like an oddity out of Madame Tussaud's. She died, at eighty-three, in 1952. The Cavendish was torn down and rebuilt as a commercial hotel. Only the name is there to remind aging roués and sprightly grandmothers of the glory that was Rosa.

177

*Top: Rosa's kitchen crew – and Louisa's (acted by Mary
Healey, Holly de Jong, and Sammie Winmill). Above: The
duchess – Gemma Jones – had her fictional Bentinck Hotel
on Duke Street, in Mayfair. Opposite: John Welsh as the butler,
Richard Vernon as major-domo, and John Cater with friend.*

Part 5

Modern Times

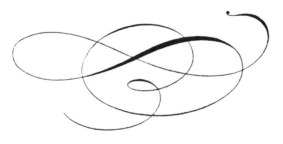

Upstairs, Downstairs

t is plain to anyone who watched much of Masterpiece Theatre in its first decade that its nucleus was the work of the BBC's drama department, during a period of great creativity. Without it, Masterpiece Theatre could hardly have existed, since American television—neither its commercial networks nor its public service—had recruited anything like such gifted teams of writers, directors, and producers, not to mention an inexhaustible supply of actors and actresses who were willing and eager to work for modest wages on the BBC's ambitious range of dramatic projects.

Yet, if Masterpiece Theatre can claim to have exhibited one television masterpiece, in the sense of a work made for television without any collateral debt to the theatre, to the cinema, or to a published work of fiction, the indisputable claimant must be *Upstairs, Downstairs,* which was created by a free-lance writer and producer for the London Weekend company and shown first on Britain's independent television network. ("Independent of what?" growled the BBC's director general when one of his staff announced he was going over to the alternative network. "Independent of the BBC, of course," the man replied.)

Upstairs, Downstairs was the chronicle of a London household existing on one of those finely graded English social strata closer to the upper than the upper-middle class, between 1903 and 1930. Through fifty-two episodes we followed the fortunes of the Richard Bellamys of Eaton Place from the imperial days of Edward the Seventh's reign through the First World War and the wrenching social changes of the 1920s to the family's abandonment of its house and the scattering of its members and staff.

It came along in the backwash of applause for the BBC's dramatized *Forsyte Saga,* and there were fears that it might founder in the wake of Galsworthy's formidable work. The fears were groundless. And what can be seen now as the tantalizing element of its success, quite independent of its intrinsic merit, was the shrewdness of its appeal to the widest possible audience. The servants of the Galsworthy households existed as lowly mechanics necessary to the maintenance of a prosperous upper-middle-class family. They were not developed as a parallel family of agonizing and rejoicing human beings. In *Upstairs, Downstairs,* both the Bellamy family and the staff were seen on their own planes in all their separate intimacy and complexity, and whenever the main story was being enacted upstairs, the downstairs team provided a counterpoint of commentary and concern. The television viewer was thus able, as he was not in the *Forsyte Saga,* to identify with the strong and whimsical humanity of the staff and, at the

*The Heart of the Matter: Hudson (Gordon Jackson),
Richard Bellamy (David Langton), James (Simon Williams),
Rose (Jean Marsh), and Mrs. Bridges (Angela Baddeley)
were the core of "Upstairs, Downstairs," which acquired
a national audience for fifty-five episodes over four seasons.*

same time, enjoy the snobbish kick of living the upstairs life. It should have been seen as a foolproof formula for ensnaring a mass audience, and undoubtedly it would have attracted one if it had been done half as well. What gave it extraordinary distinction was the sure observation of character, the confidence and finesse with which social nuances and emotional upheavals between the two groups were explored, and the scrupulous accuracy of the period language, décor, mores, and prejudices.

It is only right, then, to say how this came about, what talents were so cunningly melded into a writing and directing team. For it was a team job, a dramatic chronicle created by a dozen or so writers, five or six directors, and one producer: a rare example of a committee's producing a work of art.

The idea for the series came from Eileen Atkins and Jean Marsh (who played Rose), both of whom came from families that had been in domestic service. They wanted to show the life of a country mansion seen through the double vision of a family and its staff. They took their idea to John Hawkesworth, who seized it, substituted a town house for a country house and who, through more than four years of the making, was the producer, often the writer, and always the paterfamilias of the whole production team and acting company. He had impressive credentials for such a challenging job of social exploration, though his dossier does not at first suggest it. Reading over its early entries without any prior knowledge of his later work, or meeting him today, you would assume he had wound up as a retired brigadier general: this genial hulk of a man, sixtyish, in rumply tweeds, with a hoarfrost sparkle about him, dogs always at his heels, a brisk and competent master of fox hounds (which, in fact, he is).

He comes of a military family and was routinely sent to Rugby and Oxford. But between school and university, he had atypical ambitions. He thought of a career in architecture, he had a yearning to paint, and his father indulged him to the extent of a year in Paris where he studied under Picasso, among others, and developed a considerable talent. After Oxford, and the coming of the Second World War, he reverted to the family role and served for five years as an officer with the crack regiment of the Grenadier Guards. He found himself in the peace with a wife, no job, and no prospects. He had, however, a backlog of paintings and tried a one-man exhibition, which had the luck to be seen and admired by the Korda brothers, the film producers, who promptly hired him as a draftsman. From then on, his career was straightforward and unhalting. Very quickly promoted, he became art director (on, notably, *The Third Man*), then produced and wrote scripts for the Rank Film Company, and—when the British film industry unaccountably exhausted its postwar spurt of inventiveness—went on to television for two long writing stints, an award or two, and the decision to start his own television production company. Its first offering was *Upstairs, Downstairs*.

Every producer is duty-bound to a tedious stretch of preparation before anything can be filmed: the story line, the several drafts of the script, the reconnaissance of possible outdoor locations, the scrutiny of the art department's blueprints and much checking of proper period furniture, costumes, street lamps, automobiles, and the rest. (Hollywood has set the standard in period films for pedantic accuracy about such things as lamp shades, open-toed shoes, barroom accessories, and so forth, even when they provide the setting for improbable feelings and wildly anachronistic dialogue.) Much can be learned from Hawkesworth's research labors to explain the viewer's fascinated sense of being nowhere but in the London of 1904 or 1924. He had been a history student at Oxford, and this training, allied to an acute perception of social differences, really turned him into a social historian who had gone into television.

He began by blocking out the story line and then abandoning the script until he had scoured the period artifacts, through the microfilm file of the London *Times,* through letters, memoirs, House of Commons debates, store and fashion catalogs, weather reports, songbooks, theatre programs; noticing in passing details of contemporary slang, sporting events, deaths, reputations, best-sellers, etc. He then assembled his team of writers, assigned each episode to one or two and allowed the team the interesting freedom to bring their separate views to bear on any or all of the characters. Thus, the character of Richard Bellamy or Lady Marjorie or Rose or Hudson was never a single conception; it reflected such unexpected facets of temperament, moments of growth, as one might learn from the pooled memories of a group of friends.

The value of this dual approach, giving no license to the social and historical facts of the time, giving free play to the delineation of character, can be gauged by two examples. One was the decision to construct in minute detail a blueprint of the five-story house in which the drama was to be played. The other was the gradual emergence of a rather weak though amiable character—James Bellamy—as the moral barometer of the story and the period.

The Bellamy house, in Eaton Place, was not designed by Le Corbusier as a "machine for living." It was of the type designed by late-eighteenth-century men for the comfort and service of upper-class families. If it was a castle to such as the Bellamys, it was a gymnasium for the eighteen-hour acrobatics

183

required of the staff. They slept in the attic rooms and worked out of the basement—covering many vertical miles a day fetching and carrying. It sounds like a dog's life, but it was better than the rat's life of the mines, the factories, and what Blake called "the dark Satanic mills." Domestic service then, and for long after, provided poor people with a haven of good food, elegant surroundings, and a continuous feast of gossip. So the house was essentially a class structure, a microcosm of what its owners liked to think of as the social order, but was, in fact, a private fort protecting both Upstairs and Downstairs against the recognition of Disraeli's "two nations," the grinding rich and the ground-down poor. Hawkesworth and his writers were thoroughly at home with this ménage and its social and emotional pecking order. Unlike many professional television writers, they wrote about what they knew. And in their hands, the house and its rituals were enough to trace with absorbing and entertaining accuracy the life of one English family in one place through nearly forty years.

Many of the rewards of the preliminary social and historical research were unlocked by the decision to give Richard Bellamy, the father of the household, political ambitions. What might otherwise have been seen as an over-protected household (living, like the hero and heroine of Hollywood comedies of the 1930s, a life of intermittent quarreling and lovemaking in a vacuum of rich surroundings) was able to be subjected to a continuous wash and buffeting of events great and small, national crises, fads and festivals, the death of kings, stock market shenanigans, political scandals, the uproar of the suffragettes, the disruption of family life by the First World War, the General Strike, the coming to power of Labor governments, and eventually the Wall Street crash, the bell that tolled the end of the Bellamys' life. Out of all this, James Bellamy, the family's firstborn, emerged as the representative figure of the prime and decline of the Empire and its values, a symbol of the First World War generation at its most charming and unstable.

A few years ago, George Kennan, the American diplomat and historian, was talking about some work he was then deeply engaged in on the diplomatic history of Britain in the late nineteenth and early twentieth centuries. He mentioned some of the diplomatic material he had been plowing through. "But," he said, "I've come on one thing which shows, step by step, and more clearly and more ruthlessly than any diplomatic file, that it was the upper classes, not the lower, that cracked. And that is the television series *Upstairs, Downstairs.*" It is enough of a tribute to the firm grasp of events, to the seriousness, artfully hidden under a remarkable entertainment.

184

Family Album

Upstairs, Downstairs

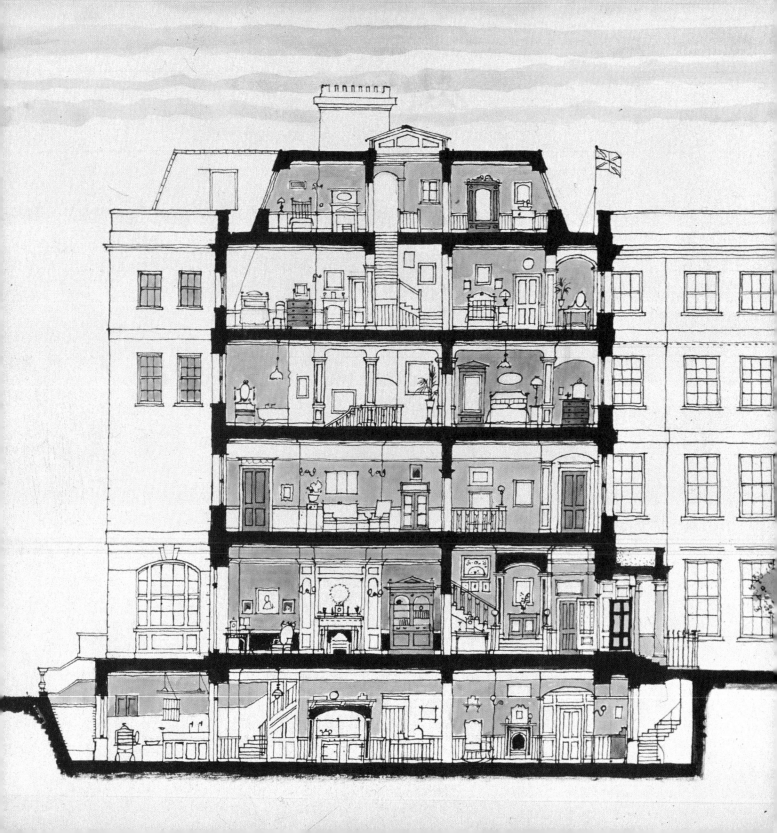

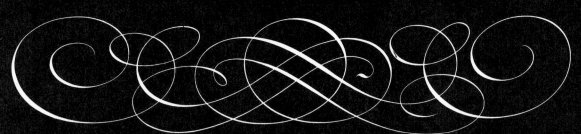

*Vertical slice through Bellamy house
at 165 Eaton Place. Front door (Hudson's
responsibility) is at right, Mrs. Bridges's
domain below stairs. Many rooms on
far side of the cut are not shown.
Above: Upstairs and Downstairs (from Series I)
sit for a proper portrait. Death of
Lady Marjorie (Rachel Gurney, seated)
brought about the first major cast change.
Below: Housemaid Daisy (Jacqueline Tong)
and her husband, Edward, the footman
(Christopher Beeny), with Hudson.*

*Opposite: Mrs. Bridges and Rose give
high-calorie desserts a final inspection
before sending them upstairs to
grace the Bellamy's holiday table. Below:
Edward and Rose attend a royal guest,
King Edward VII (Lockwood West).
Right: Sir Arthur Stockdale Cope's portrait
of His Majesty, 1907. Aside from the
accuracy of its social microcosm
and its acutely observed people, the show
derived much of its brilliance from
Richard's career in politics. Upstairs and
Downstairs were involved in the world
without, as well as the one within.*

189

Family gathering in the Bellamy drawing room. Next to Richard is daughter Elizabeth (Nicola Pagett). She departs to marry a Canadian, and Lady Marjorie (right) will die in an accident on a journey to see her. At her right is gossipy Aunt Prue (Joan Benham). Jean Marsh (Rose, above and opposite) and a colleague originated the idea of the show. Left: Hudson and Mrs. Bridges. The formality of their relationship as butler and cook occasionally was breached by their warm, human regard for each other. Angela Baddeley died soon after the series ended.

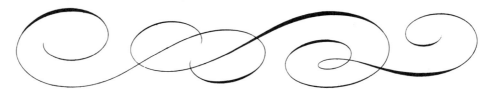

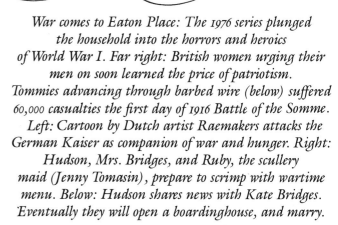

War comes to Eaton Place: The 1976 series plunged the household into the horrors and heroics of World War I. Far right: British women urging their men on soon learned the price of patriotism. Tommies advancing through barbed wire (below) suffered 60,000 casualties the first day of 1916 Battle of the Somme. Left: Cartoon by Dutch artist Raemakers attacks the German Kaiser as companion of war and hunger. Right: Hudson, Mrs. Bridges, and Ruby, the scullery maid (Jenny Tomasin), prepare to scrimp with wartime menu. Below: Hudson shares news with Kate Bridges. Eventually they will open a boardinghouse, and marry.

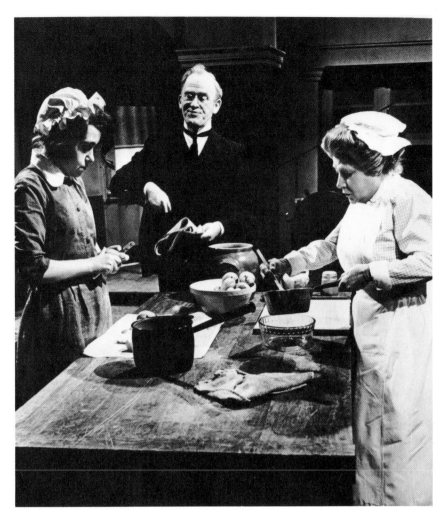

As the war deepened, the Bellamy household (top left) turned to. Georgina became a nurse, Ruby worked in a munitions factory, Rose became a street car conductor. Edward and James went to war in different regiments, of course. James was severely wounded at Passchendaele (below, right). Hudson (on phone) was rejected and, fuming, became a special constable. Rose's fiancé, Mr. Wilmot, joined Downstairs at table (top right), was later missing in action. Opposite: Christmas together. James's wife Hazel (Meg Wynn Owen) will die in flu epidemic.

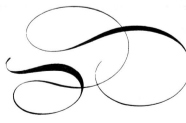

*Celebrating the Twenties: In the 1977 series the
household enjoys the return of peace and prosperity.
But times are changing. The context of life
in prewar Britain is vanishing and Eaton Place is
becoming an anachronism. Signs and portents, opposite:
Rudolph Valentino and John Held Jr.'s
flapper symbolized the rising power of the movies
and the hedonism of the Jazz Age. James and
Georgina (Lesley-Anne Down) do the Charleston, while
Rose, Mrs. Bridges, and Ruby, in appropriate
costume, enjoy the seaside. Left: Henry Ford, in his
first car, advanced the revolution in transport with
cheap cars. Goggled James and Hudson take a
spin in a sports runabout.*

As the '29 crash nears: Up and Down sit for a final portrait (opposite). Seated are Georgina, Richard, his calm second wife, Virginia (Hannah Gordon), and ill-starred James, for whom nothing goes very well. New stepchildren are on the floor. Standing, from left, are Daisy, Ruby, Edward, Rose, Hudson, Mrs. Bridges, Frederick (Gareth Hunt), and Lily (Karen Dotrice). Above left: Georgina marries. Her husband is played by Anthony Andrews. Above: Angus Hudson visits his beloved Scotland, in series IV. Right: Ruby, packed and ready, as Eaton Place is emptied of its old life.

The resurrection on television of any forgotten book, whether a masterpiece or a simple yarn, obviously exposes it to an audience vaster than any reading public and is likely to promote a fame the original never enjoyed. What, I think, is more interesting about *Testament of Youth* is that whether or not it stirred the same complex of emotions in the viewers of 1980 as it did in the readers of 1933, its political and psychological appeal to a modern audience was quite different from its appeal to the British and American readers of fifty years ago.

It is part of an autobiography, the memoir of a young Englishwoman's experience of the First World War, published fifteen years after it was over. When it came out in 1933, Vera Brittain was an established but minor English novelist in her thirty-eighth year. Her book was warmly received. It was called "haunting," "sensitive," "full of gallantry and pathos." But it was by no means a literary bombshell. Robert Graves lumped it with G. D. H. Coles's *Europe Today,* Edgar Mowrer's *Germany Puts the Clock Back,* and Vernon Bartlett's *Nazi Germany Explained,* as a symptom of the unease that was overtaking Europeans and Americans about the apparent failure of "collective security" and the growing fear of a second World War. There may be old people today who can claim to have been moved in a particular way by Vera Brittain's memoir, but at the time it was seen as a late contribution to a literature of disillusion by readers who had had their fill of "war is hell" books.

It took some time after the war, however, for the debunking war books to appear, and another three or four years before the appetite for them was cloyed. The memoirs of participating statesmen and generals, reviving old political jousts and defending old positions, had not yet started to disturb the peace. In the 1920s, war literature, such as it was during a general and willing retreat into romantic fiction, belles lettres, American musical comedy, and other forms of escapism, was written mostly by old soldiers bringing regimental histories up to date, and by former war correspondents celebrating the heroism of famous battles, the valor of the ordinary soldier, and recalling "how fine a thing was the fighting fellowship."

The reaction set in when, in 1929, from Germany came the thunderclap of Erich Maria Remarque's *All Quiet on the Western Front,* which was all the more powerful for its absence of protest or, indeed, of any conscious "reaction" against the previous spate of patriotic reminiscences. In a tone of uncomplaining resignation, it showed the ordinary German soldier to be as frightened, as stoical, as exhausted, as immune to heroics, as his enemy, the British

Tommy. The British followed very soon with stronger, more polemical stuff: Richard Aldington's *Death of a Hero*, C. E. Montague's *Disenchantment*, Robert Graves's *Goodbye to All That*. The resounding London theatre success of the 1929–30 season was R. C. Sheriff's *Journey's End*, which converted the stage into a dugout on the Western front and explored the mixed emotions of men who were stuck in it like rats in a cellar. As in most other war stories, there were no women in the cast. And that may be the clue to our present interest in *Testament of Youth*.

The incentive to revive it must have come not from someone's renewed interest in the First World War but from the current Western overhaul of the status of women. If this memoir had been adapted twenty years ago, it would certainly have had a different emotional emphasis, a more conventional dramatic bent. As it was, the dramatization was suggested by a woman, undertaken by the novelist, Elaine Morgan, and directed by another woman, Moira Armstrong. Its reception was startling in its spontaneity and range. It won every sort of television prize in Britain and Europe, and a torrent of mail attested to the fact that it had moved a new generation of young women who were fifty years away from the original work and nearly seventy years away from what it was all about.

The line of the memoir is simple and its tragedy unrelenting. Vera Brittain was the daughter of a prosperous North country mill owner, a self-made man presiding over a household of stifling gentility from which Vera, a dutiful but intellectual girl, yearns to escape. Against the father's proud plan to have his only daughter rise, through the debutante route, to a social position his family has never aspired to, Vera sticks to her own plan to go, along with her brother, to Oxford. To the father, it is a galling defeat, to the daughter a leap to freedom. She passes the preliminary examinations, enters an Oxford college, and falls in love with her brother's best friend. A dreamy summer, of literary argument and romantic by-play, is shattered by the guns of August 1914. "I had made for myself," she wrote, "a way of escape from my hated provincial prison, and now the road to freedom was to be closed for me by some Serbian bomb hurled from the other end of Europe at an Austrian archduke. . . . It is not perhaps so very surprising that the war at first seemed to me an infuriating personal interruption rather than what it became, a worldwide catastrophe."

It was not so petulant a response as we might think it today. Vera Brittain was only three when the Boer War broke out, and the British hadn't fought on the continent of Europe for the better part of a century. But once her brother and her fiancé were away in France, her intellectual life was meaningless,

and the social life at home an exacerbation of her sense of impotence. She enlisted as a nurse in a military hospital in London. Three days before her fiancé was to come home on leave, he died of wounds. Shortly afterward, her brother was wounded and returned home, to be comforted by his sister and two other soldier friends. The badinage of these three, and the prospect of its being only a brief brave interlude in the general slaughter, was too much for Vera. She applied for overseas service and was posted to a hospital in Malta. There she learned that one of the soldier friends had been killed and the other, whom she later decided to marry, had been blinded. In the last year of the war, she was called home from a hospital in France to nurse a sick mother and receive the ultimate blow that her brother had been killed in Italy.

Vera Brittain (Cheryl Campbell) and her beloved, Roland Leighton (Peter Woodward). In the first patriotic flush of World War I, he transfers to a regiment that is leaving early for the front and becomes the first of four young men in her life to die in action.

Few families in Britain or Europe were lucky enough to count no casualties among their sons and lovers, but if this had been a novel, I think it would have been discredited for too much piling of grief onto one person. But because it was a true account, and because all the war books had been written by men about the agonies of the battlefront, with the implication that it was woman's role to wait and mourn, Vera Brittain's memoir of a devastated youth brought into pitiful relief the ordeals of war that are peculiar to women everywhere.

Not surprisingly, Vera Brittain became an ardent pacifist and feminist. Along with Aldous Huxley, she was one of the founding members of the Peace Pledge Union, which by 1937 had canvassed 130,000 signatures of ordinary citizens pledged to "renounce war." How these fine people, who would be the last to be consulted about national policy, were going to do this was never practically defined. But the movement held immense rallies and organized study groups whose aim was to urge on the colonial powers the liberation of their wards, on the Nazis the virtues of scientific agriculture as a peaceful alternative to the pressure for "living room," and on everybody the voluntary abolition of nationalism. Vera Brittain carried her proselytizing to Europe and the United States until it was vitiated by the invasion of Poland. Not the least, however, of her political legacies is her daughter, Shirley Williams, the only woman Cabinet minister in the last Labor government and one of the "gang of four" that recently broke away from the Labor Party and formed the new Social Democratic Party in Britain.

That *Testament of Youth* can be sympathetically regarded quite outside the context of Women's Lib, or any other feminist frame, is demonstrated in the most remarkable review that I have come across. It is a notice in *Punch,* in September 1933, in which a male reviewer makes the (to us) premature assumption that women are equal citizens, to be called on for an equal show of courage. The other assumption, sustaining the first (and one which today would probably cross the mind only of the most religious) is that people, men and women alike, need in hard times a faith to see them through:

The cataclysm of 1914 found Miss Vera Brittain one of a close-knit circle which included a devoted brother and three of his comrades-in-arms. By 1918 all were gone except the girl; and she, having toiled her heart out at hospital work in England, Malta and France, with neither faith enough to sanction exaltation nor doubt enough for effective defiance, went back to her work at Oxford, and on via the League to international Socialism. It is impossible to condemn a nursling of nineteenth-century materialism for having failed to improvise a creed which should see her through the shattering of her world.

Dorothy Sayers

Clouds of Witness   Murder Must Advertise   The Unpleasantness at the Bellona Club
The Nine Tailors   Five Red Herrings

The origin of the mystery thriller is an inquiry well worth forgoing. It would encourage a posse of literary sleuths and probably involve us in arguments about late-eighteenth-century Gothic tales, and Horace Walpole, and "riddle stories" going back to Samson. The encyclopedias threaten us with the reminder that "its seeds are found in the folklore of the oldest nations."

But there is no quarrel about who planted the seed of the detective thriller. Dorothy Sayers herself adds her tribute to the findings of the scholars. Poe's *Murders in the Rue Morgue,* she says, "constitutes almost a complete manual of detective theory and practice." It came out in 1841, only a few years after the profession of detective was invented. Poe wrote three detective stories in all, and after him came the first detective writer to make a full-time job of it: Emile Gaboriau, who created Lecocq. (Poe and Gaboriau, Conan Doyle was to say, were his only models.) Two years after Gaboriau, the fashion passed to England, and Wilkie Collins produced, in *The Moonstone,* the first full-length detective novel in English.

204

Collins was a London journalist who started to contribute short mystery stories to a magazine edited by his close friend, Charles Dickens. Quite suddenly, he erupted in *The Moonstone,* and as suddenly was famous. Considered as the hundred-year-old ancestor of the modern detective story, it is an astonishing novelty. It has most of the elements we expect to find in a contemporary work: the missing object, the many suspects, the obtuse cop, the effortlessly superior detective. One other element, which may now seem old-fashioned and farfetched,. was undoubtedly the topical note that spiced public interest. The story was set in 1848, the year in which the Punjab became the first Indian province to pass under the dominion of the British Crown. To signify the surrender of the Punjab's sovereignty, the Maharajah presented to Queen Victoria a huge diamond, the Koh-I-Noor, $186\frac{1}{16}$ carats. For many years it was the talk of the country and the daydream of every duchess with a presentable chest, a hope chest, that is. In Collins's fictional adaptation, the moonstone is a giant yellow diamond stolen from the statue of an Indian god by an English soldier during a siege in Southern India.

After Collins, the hereditary line of the detective thriller passes through Anna Katherine Green (*The Leavenworth Case*), in America, Fergus Hume (*The Mystery of a Hansom Cab*), in Australia, and returns with an historic flourish to London, to Conan Doyle and Sherlock Holmes. After him, the deluge.

First detective in English fiction was Sergeant Cuff
(John Welsh, far right) in "The Moonstone." Betteredge the
butler (Basil Dignam) and maid (Vivian Heilbron, left)
were involved. Dorothy L. Sayers (top) created Lord Peter
Wimsey, center, below, in "Murder Must Advertise."

Of the dozen or so contemporary writers who have become masters of the field, including Agatha Christie, Dorothy Leigh Sayers is the most improbable recruit. On short acquaintance, you would have expected her to be the sort of intellectual—like Bertrand Russell—who put interviewers at their ease by confessing a sneaking addiction to whodunits. She died in 1957 at the age of sixty-four and ended her career where she began it, as a medieval and theological historian. Her father was a Victorian clergyman, the headmaster of a cathedral school, who departed for a country rectory along with his four-year-old daughter, a nurse, a maiden aunt, and a parrot. When Dorothy was seven, he decided she was old enough to start Latin, and while still a child she spoke it almost as fluently as, in her teens, she spoke French and German. She was one of the first women to graduate from Oxford and was certainly the first with a first-class honors degree in medieval literature. She started to teach German, until the First

"Clouds of Witness" was the first television presentation of Sayers's work. Above: Lord Peter (Ian Carmichael) receives help from his man Bunter (Glyn Houston). Opposite: Mr. Murbles (John Welsh) and Pritchard (Clifford Rose) consider "The Unpleasantness at the Bellona Club."

World War put an abrupt end to the Victorian and Edwardian devotion to all things German. She turned to religious poetry, published a small volume of it, and then in the first startling turn of her career joined the biggest British advertising company as a copywriter. It was a two-year stint that left her with a bilious view of the advertising world and enough knowing material to incorporate years later in her very tart novel about the decadent 1920s (*Murder Must Advertise*), the closest she came in her lighthearted profession to a social satire.

An industrious and inquisitive young woman, very much the child of a Victorian enthusiast, she employed her spare time maintaining her interest in theology but also delving in her scholarly fashion into an assortment of specialities—music, church architecture, medicine, archeology, law-court procedure, the history of wines, the techniques of bell ringing (*The Nine Tailors*), and of painters and painting (*Five Red Herrings*), the nuances of club life (*The Unpleas-*

antness at the Bellona Club). Her particular hobby was the expensive one of collecting incunabula, and she hadn't the money to pursue it. She decided to get some. And that is how Lord Peter Wimsey was born.

Her first novel (*Whose Body?*) didn't catch on, and at the age of twenty-three, she had painful second thoughts, assuaged no doubt by her marriage to a dashing soldier, Captain Oswald Atherton Fleming. If he ever had the satisfying thought that he had given a boost to a disappointed ego, he was in for an early shock. Captain Fleming very soon had to be content to be known as Mr. Dorothy Sayers, for in the year she married him, 1926, she had a second try and sat down to write *Clouds of Witness*. It was an immediate success and started a Wimsey vogue that lasted long after she had killed him off. It was to guarantee her, for the pursuit of her hobby and her study of medieval saints, the royalties from thirteen million copies of her remaining work. The popularity of *Clouds of Witness* was due, we must assume, to the recognition of a sharp and ingenious intelligence exercising itself on a completely new type of detective whose noble lineage and upper-crust habits were calculated to recruit a new and snobbish clientele for detective stories. In a funny and perceptive essay, Carolyn Heilbrun says: "The [creation] of the Duke of Denver, Lord Peter's brother, as the richest peer in England [was] a stroke of genius. It is a frightful nuisance if one's detec-

Art mixes with murder in "Five Red Herrings" (left).
Ferguson, the artist, is played by David McKail. In "The Nine
Tailors" (right), a cipher based on the patterns of
bell-ringers' changes is cracked by Lord Peter and the Rev.
Mr. Venables (Donald Eccles) and leads to the Wilbraham emeralds.

tive, with no police department funds behind him, has to cavil over minor matters such as setting up an entire establishment of female detectives or hiring a plane to fly the Atlantic. It was either luck or cunning foresight that made Dorothy Sayers invent this last absurdity, which was amazingly realized by Lindbergh only after Lord Peter had blazed the trail in order to save his brother from a conviction for murder by the only court qualified to try a noble lord, namely, the House of Lords.

Both the plot and the social atmosphere of *Clouds of Witness* revived the imagined grandeur and serenity of a world that had been shattered by the First World War. The detective thriller, the crossword puzzle, and American jazz all came along at the same time, in the early 1920s, as anodynes against the facts of unemployment in Britain, famine and revolution in Europe, and a moral upheaval among the young. A fantasy world of private detectives mushroomed in fiction, intense and all-knowing men invariably investigating murders that bore no resemblance to the crimes that confronted the police. It got to the point, wrote Robert Graves, where "the crime could have been committed only by someone with a knowledge of Chinese, in desperate need of money, who could persuade a left-handed Negro dwarf to train a monkey to climb up a ventilator pipe and squirt a rare South American poison into the victim's hot bath—with a syringe through the keyhole—at the one short moment when the French maid's back was turned."

On the contrary, Dorothy Sayers wrote, "I wanted to make a detective story a novel of manners rather than a crossword puzzle." The invention of Lord Peter was a pledge for her later work that whatever the plot, its manners would offer a delicious and prolonged tour of the manor house to us gaping visitors from the pale of the middle class. This condescension could have been boring in less expert hands. But the character of Lord Peter himself was the unique attraction. He knew everything, as Sherlock Holmes did, but with a quite new, worldly, and off-handed sprightliness. He was right out of P. G. Wodehouse on the surface, right out of Raymond Chandler underneath: Bertie Wooster with Bogart's brain. It was a formula that enriched Dorothy Sayers and her estate for nearly fifty years.

After the Second World War, she abandoned detective, and every other sort of, fiction. She made an English translation of the first part of Dante's *Inferno* and after an unhappy marriage returned with new fervor to her Anglican faith and the propagation of it in two missionary works: *Begin Here* and *Creed or Chaos?*

Somerset Maugham
Cakes and Ale

Whether he was in London, Bangkok, San Francisco, or the south of France, Somerset Maugham burned no midnight oil. By the dawn's early light, he was sound asleep. Everywhere, he led an active social life. In his Riviera villa, he never missed his noon cocktail, he took a social lunch, an afternoon nap, and a social dinner, and was usually free in the evenings for long sessions of bridge. To an incredulous guest who asked him how he managed to produce a substantial body of work, he gave the pro's classic answer: "After breakfast I go to my desk, seven days a week, and nothing interferes with my writing for the next three hours. It is enough."

William Somerset Maugham was born in Paris, in 1874, the son of a lawyer attached to the British Embassy. He learned to speak French before English and when he went home to school in England, an orphan of ten, he was mocked for his mispronunciations, a routine cruelty which he maintained took its toll in a lifelong stammer. It may also, though, have sharpened a defensive talent for irony and strengthened his sympathy for simple or rebellious people who found themselves up against confident social types.

Debonair Somerset Maugham, white-gloved, stiff-collared, and grey-toppered, regards us coolly from Sir Gerald Kelly's 1911 portrait, "The Jester." Left: Warm-hearted barmaid Rosie (Judy Cornwell) beguiles young Willie Ashenden (Paul Aston), the Maugham-like narrator of "Cakes and Ale."

After a year at school in Germany, he went into medical school, and in the year of his graduation published a first novel, *Liza of Lambeth,* which incorporated the few pleasures and many pains of caring for the sick in a very poor part of London. (He drew on the same experiences later in *Of Human Bondage.*) He traveled widely in Europe, turned to playwriting and was very soon a resounding commercial success. After a spell as a secret agent during the First World War, he traveled around the world, wrote many short stories based— often literally—on newspaper stories he picked up, and in his early fifties settled in the south of France.

Cakes and Ale, which has withstood the ups and downs of his reputation, is a compact satire on the fame of a grand old man of English literature and a biographer who hopes to batten on it. The nub of the story is the discrepancy between the facts of the old man's life and the preconceived fancies of the biographer. He wants the "life" to come out dignified and stately, to lament its hero's early marriage to a trollop and show him moving into his maturity under the influence of a dignified and sensitive second wife. The narrator (Maugham) is an old friend of the great man's and delights in riling the biographer with the embarrassing facts: such as, that the old man had lived a homely, raunchy life, that his second wife was a pretentious nag, that his first wife—a cheerful barmaid, free with her favors—was a generous and good human being.

The book set off a scandal when it appeared in 1930. It is an almost shameless *roman à clef.* The grand old man was plainly and vividly no one but Thomas Hardy (who had recently died), for all Maugham's protestations that he might just as well have had in mind Tennyson or Meredith. But if Hardy hadn't crossed Maugham's mind, the character of the wheedling biographer was instantly recognizable to the literary world as a cruel caricature of the novelist Hugh Walpole. Much later, Maugham broke down and admitted that Walpole was indeed the victim: "I had no wish to hurt him, he was a genial creature and he had friends who, though they were apt to laugh at him, were genuinely attached to him. He was easy to like but difficult to admire." Maugham, in turning this belated compliment, did not fail to turn the knife in the wound.

Without doubt, *Cakes and Ale* is a work of malice, directed not only against its two monster characters but against the British literary establishment, which, by 1930, had grown weary of Maugham and began to belittle him as an aging and mechanical cynic. It is embarrassing to have to say that, like some other venomous works, such as Dryden's *Absalom and Achitophel,* Pope's *Essay On Man,* Evelyn Waugh's *Vile Bodies, Cakes and Ale* is, nevertheless, a small

masterpiece. As a human document, the redeeming element—as it is in many of Maugham's stories—is the author's insistence on the kindness and warmth of the lowliest character, in this work the slighted barmaid.

The ebb and flow in the reputation of any writer who lives to a great age (Maugham died at ninety-one) is always historically interesting, if only as a gauge marking the shifts of literary fashion. Maugham is the specially interesting case of a writer whose popularity was, from early middle age on, the constant foe of his literary reputation. It is a plight so familiar in this century that we tend to forget how new it is. The popularity of Dickens, Balzac, Scott, Tolstoy, Flaubert did not call in to question their literary merit. Balzac's jewels and Dickens's gaudy clothes did not prevent their owners being taken seriously. The people took their cue from the critics, and the critics—though probably just as subject then as now to second thoughts and simple envy of creative writers—did not feel their judgment challenged by the applause of the masses. Between then and now, however, a new arbiter has appeared on the literary scene.

A useful year to fix on as an omen for Maugham is 1908. He was then thirty-four, four of his plays were having long runs in London, and they

*Rosie, frolicking with pub regulars, turns out to
have been the cheerful first wife of a grand old man of
English letters whose life was wildly at odds with
his biographer's preconceptions. Maugham confessed that his
model for the smarmy biographer was Hugh Walpole.*

gave him financial security once for all. It was also the year when a new word slipped into the literary and aesthetic vocabulary: the word "highbrow," which first appeared in print in the United States. It passed into popular parlance on both sides of the Atlantic in the next twenty years, and it is merely the most conspicuous sign of the arrival of a fourth man, claiming to adjudicate among the writer, the reviewers, and his readers. The judgment of contemporary work in many fields—in fiction, drama, history, biography, science, movies (especially)—has been bedeviled ever since by the anxiety of the highbrow to find merit only in what is difficult or *recherché* and to steel himself against the preferences of the masses. This figure, the high priest guarding the oracles, appeared in its most imperious form in the early thirties in the person of the Cambridge don, F. R. Leavis. He and his wife wrote *Fiction and the Reading Public,* which deplored urban life, advertising, radio, the movies, politics, best-sellers, and popular fiction, the whole apparatus of mass civilization, as a barbarian threat to the besieged fort of "minority culture." The culture of the minority, as defined by Dr. Leavis, soon came to be reduced to those very few authors of whom he approved: T. S. Eliot, Gerard Manley Hopkins, D. H. Lawrence. (This assumption of godhead had its comical side. I myself came very briefly under the wing, never the spell, of Dr. Leavis. When I was asked about my general reading and mentioned a passion for Dickens, the good doctor—of philosophy—was deeply pained. When I added a taste for Maugham's short stories, I was dismissed and unfrocked. Ten years or so later, Dr. Leavis announced to a shocked world that Dickens was a genius of the first order and must be read at once. He never, I believe, sank to an enjoyment of Maugham.)

  I believe, then, that Maugham, dismissed by highbrows as a naive cynic and derided by academics wholly unfamiliar with the world he wrote about, is to be seen as an upper-middle-class Edwardian who, by the early luck of his doctor's training in a London slum and his lifelong taste for traveling to the far corners of the earth, developed in a simple—sometimes an oversimple—style a distrustful view of powerful people, a wry interest in the discomfort of Englishmen in an alien culture, and a preoccupation with the evasions of people of his class before the simple people who served them. The reader should beware of dismissing him too glibly. Between Edmund Wilson's case for the prosecution that he is "a half-trashy novelist who writes badly" and George Orwell's defense of him as a master, "the modern writer who has influenced me most," the jury is still out.

213

If Herbert Ernest Bates had not been twenty-seven years younger than his mentor, A. E. Coppard, the two of them could have set up a firm: Coppard & Bates, Purveyors of Rural Life. Both were born poor, both were engrossed by a region of the English countryside and settled in it, both shunned the social traffic of the successful writer, and both lived modestly till the end of their days, in what Bates called "country self-sufficiency." And both, therefore, came to be taken at their own valuation, as minor practitioners of the short story on rural themes. Today, like most writers half a century or so from the time and place they wrote about, they exist in that limbo that is perilous for the reputation of authors both great and small; they are just too far from our daily lives to provoke vivid recognition, not far enough to be rescued as fascinating antiques. Yet their stories—those of Bates especially—take such a grip on unchanging themes—first love, betrayal, self-righteousness, stoicism in adversity—that they appear to write, though in a fading idiom, with absolute sureness about country and provincial life of any time.

Alfred Edgar Coppard was born in Kent, in 1879, to a chambermaid and a tubercular father, a tailor, whose death left the nine-year-old boy destitute and at the end of all the formal education he was to have. For the next twenty years, he padded though an interminable variety of menial jobs—errand boy, warehouse boy, grocery clerk—including some so alien to our century that they sound like low-character occupations in an Elizabethan comedy: one was "street vendor of paraffin."

From boyhood on, he retained two passions. He begged or borrowed every book in sight, and when he wasn't bent over them indoors he was outdoors running on the South Downs. For ten years, indeed, he was a well-known sprinter in various parts of the country and soaked up the juices of the landscape and the people who lived on it. In his thirtieth year, he got a job as an accountant in an ironworks in, of all places, Oxford. That may sound improbable to an intending tourist, but when, early in the century, factories began to smoke in the countryside of Southern England, Oxford failed to act on the foresight of Cambridge, which passed a local ordinance forbidding industry to come closer than eleven miles. On the contrary, the Oxford that Coppard knew had printing and ironworks, in 1912 an automobile factory, and very shortly was a center of the steel and electrical engineering industries. But the university was there too, and in the evenings Coppard fell in with undergraduate literary types, with Aldous Huxley and L. A. G. Strong and Richard Hughes.

Coppard (top left) was Bates's mentor in style, genre, and reclusiveness. Top right: In "Crippled Bloom," Pauline Collins (left) loses Joss Ackland to her sister Anna Cropper. Above: Glyn Houston and Jane Lapotaire are an embittered father and daughter in "The Black Dog."

Unlike other poor-boy authors, he was not put out by this exposure to the upper and upper-middle classes. He looked on them neither as enemies nor as people he ought to pretend to know about. He remained a sympathetic outsider, preserved from sycophancy by striking good looks, a strong sardonic vein, and a flourish of cranky opinions. Thomas Hardy remained his favorite novelist and Thackeray his abomination.

He had a long struggle getting published. His first stories came out when he was in his early forties, but once he left Oxford and retreated for good to the country, he acquired a small and faithful readership, possibly more cynical than the wider audience for Bates, since Coppard, even in a real and fictional world dominated by conservative provincial types, by farmers linked to the fortune of their crops, by the intrigue and gossip of a market town, did not mask his proclaimed identity as "a socialist and a materialist, with an instinctive dislike of parsons, policemen and military." He may have mellowed toward the end (he died at seventy-nine in 1957) but not sufficiently to recant his ideal of conduct: "To do unto others what ought to have been done unto them long ago."

Bates's early life is almost a predestined copy of Coppard's though nothing like so bleak for so long. He was born in Northamptonshire, in 1905, in the harsh countryside that fringes the Midlands' industrial towns. His father was

Above: Peter Firth, Penelope Wilton (standing), and Claire Sutcliffe in Coppard's "The Sullens Sisters." Opposite: Bates's "Breeze Anstey" (top) featured Morag Hood and Meg Wynn Owen. In "An Aspidistra in Babylon," Carolyn Courage is the lover of an officer (Jeremy Brett).

*Bucolic milieus like Castle Combe (opposite)
were the world of Coppard and Bates. Scenes from "Love for
Lydia": Lydia (Mel Martin) makes another conquest
(Jeremy Irons), and Beatrix Lehmmann (left) and Rachel Kempson
as her eccentric aunts. Right: Bates, on location.*

a shoemaker with the single hobby of walking with his young son, winter and summer, through the motorless roads, the towpaths, the blackberry hedges, the small woods. "Out of this unprepossessing midland earth," Bates wrote, "sprang all my feelings and love of the countryside." He took a free place at a grammar school, left it at sixteen, became a newspaper reporter and loathed it. He went into a warehouse as a packer, evidently a lazy packer and a quick one, for he boasted that he often had most of the day left to write short stories on the company time. When he was twenty he was unemployed, on relief, and hawking a novel round London. Nine publishers turned it down, and the tenth gave him the undreamed-of advance of twenty-five pounds.

During his early twenties, his publisher's reader, Edward Garnett, told him his stuff was "Thomas Hardy with water" and made him destroy or rewrite and rewrite. He found himself in the early 1930s retired to a cottage and in the next forty-odd years put out seventy volumes of fiction and essays. (In the Second World War, he broke away for the duration from "country self-sufficiency," was commissioned as an official army writer, became a squadron leader in the Royal Air Force, and, under the pseudonym of Flying Officer X, wrote his only best-seller, *Fair Stood the Wind for France,* the story of a bomber pilot brought down in France and saved by the local country people.)

The longest of his stories to be dramatized for television (in twelve episodes) was *Love for Lydia,* a chronicle of the fortunes of a small factory town planted in farming country in the Midlands, and of the effect on its middle-class mores of the arrival of the young heiress to a factory fortune. A languid, taunting girl, Lydia is always just ahead of her neighbors in acquiring the nervous sophistication of the 1920s, its fads and frivolities, but Bates, a romantic puritan, plots for her a doom, through tuberculosis, that parallels the decay of the town as it moves out of the era of wonderful nonsense into the despair of the great Depression. It is a slow, bitter, relentless tale, Hardy with gall and wormwood, but Bates's sympathy for even the most feckless characters is unwavering. Henry Miller, an unlikely convert to stories so grave and placid, thought of Bates as his favorite writer of fiction and has put his finger on three qualities most characteristic of him: "An uncanny insight into women; an extraordinary eye for the physical world; and a strong belief that the supreme mark of the hero is the ability to endure pain."

Most of the time, in Bates, we are in the presence, as somebody else said, of people "to whom pleasure and tragedy are homely things: the heart adapts—and copes."

Richard Llewellyn
How Green Was My Valley

Of all the humble trades that have been celebrated in poetry, fiction, and painting—the shepherd, the soldier, the sailor, the cowboy, the farmer, the blacksmith—the coal miner must be the one who least lends himself to romantic contemplation. Certainly the life of the coal miner is something to be recollected in a bitter mixture of hostility and tenderness, and then only by sons, like D. H. Lawrence, who escape from it, or by propaganda muralists, like Diego Rivera, who use it as a symbol of servitude. In *Kameradschaft (Comradeship)* the German director G. W. Pabst gave an heroic dimension to the hardship of the miner's life by showing how pride of craft dissolved national animosities during a cave-in on the Franco-German border.

For the rest, all the main films on the subject have been about Britain. Hollywood has approached the plight of American miners in a gingerly fashion, though *Black Fury* was a plucky 1930s' effort to dramatize the problems of safety and union organization. By far the most successful of Hollywood's few films about miners was *How Green Was My Valley,* but its success was contrived by unrelieved sentimentality and the casting of a handful of established stars whose resemblance to Welsh mining folk was, except for Sara Allgood, barely plausible.

However, the novel on which the film was based is another thing. It is the work of Richard Dafydd Vivian Llewellyn Lloyd, who sensibly took his first and fourth given names as his pen name. He was born in Cardiff, in 1907,

Richard Llewellyn wrote "How Green Was My Valley"
in India, while serving with the British army. Although he
eventually produced twenty-one novels, this authentic
and deeply felt story of the grinding life of the
Welsh coal mines remained his best-known work.

and brought up among coal miners until his seventeenth year, when he had what must have been a unique experience for a boy of his upbringing: he was sent off to Italy to learn hotel management. It was not a speciality that appealed to him. He was a restless boy with vague artistic yearnings, but after a little dabbling in painting and sculpture, he quit the arts for the British army, in which he served at home and abroad for five years. As so often happens when an impressionable writer is far from his roots, Llewellyn returned to them in imagination with passionately detailed recall. It was in India that he wrote the first draft of *How Green Was My Valley*. He left the army in the trough of the Depression and during several jobless stretches he rewrote his story, partly at home in Cardiff, partly on a bench in London's St. James's Park. On and off, he worked as an extra in British movies and as a director, until he was fired. The completed novel was accepted just before the outbreak of the Second World War. It was a re-sounding hit. He celebrated his first taste of good fortune in the army again and served throughout the war as a captain in the Welsh Guards. When it was over, he devoted himself exclusively to fiction and wrote twenty-one novels. But, except among readers of *None but the Lonely Heart,* a moody story about a Cockney drifter, he has had to endure the general reputation of a one-book author.

222

Nothing he wrote can match *How Green Was My Valley* in authenticity and directness of feeling. It contains characters who, if only from literary neglect, are too exotic to readers and moviegoers to be recognized as stereotypes; but they are familiar enough as immemorial types to the inhabitants of mining villages. There is the gritty patriarch and the submissive mother; the rebellious son, a union organizer contemptuous of his father's acceptance of the miners' working conditions; the deacon, an Old Testament bigot wreaking vengeance, as God's stand-in, on a pregnant girl; the prissy, English-trained schoolmaster affecting pain at his pupils' lapses into Welsh; the frail scholar of a son whose father dares to see him as the first of the family who might flee the prison of the mines through the escape-hatch of education; and the proud daughter who goes over to the enemy by marrying the mine owner's son, an uppity Oxford type who wants to sever all connection with coal mining except the income he derives from it.

It sounds already like "strong" Hollywood material. However, three qualities of this BBC version gave it a harsh, at times heartbreaking, verisimilitude: the actual location in a Welsh mining village, as against the mimic Hollywood set; the personal experience of the scriptwriter and the leading actors—practically unique in any film or television play—with the life and landscape of

Top: The Morgans, and son Ianto (Keith Drinkel), the strong union man. Middle: The late Stanley Baker as Gwilym Morgan (left) and Dominic Guard as Huw. Bottom: The Rev. Mr. Gruffyd (Gareth Thomas) with young Huw (Rhys Powys) and sister Angharad (Sue Jones-Davies).

the characters portrayed; and, always as a menacing presence in the background, the history of the miners and the hazards of their trade.

Elaine Morgan, who wrote the television script, is the daughter of a colliery pumpman and drew on the diaries of her father-in-law, another miner, that go back to 1896. All the leading actors were born in Wales. Of the two stars, Sian Phillips, who played the mother, spoke nothing but Welsh till she was sixteen, and the late Stanley Baker, the father, was the son of a miner who lost a leg in a cave-in. Both of them worked with mixed feelings among the scenes of their childhood: a segregated world of men down the pits and up in the pubs, and the tighter world still of the housewives waiting for the knock-off whistle with one ear always cocked for the sound of a siren. It was, said Baker, still "a place where death and poverty are daily threats."

The period of the story is the 1890s, but it might just as well have been 1790 or, in some rude fundamentals, 1290. For they were digging coal in South Wales seven hundred years ago. Miners in any country have always been a race apart. In Wales, they were for centuries isolated from England and even from their own city people by the language, and—as they are today—by deep narrow valleys which hem them in between the mountains. The crests of the hills are lined with trolleys, and wherever there is level ground, it is grey with cones of slag heaps.

In the 1890s, South Wales was the chief coal-exporting region of the world, because of its superior coal, which is dry and fiery. By a doleful irony, the

Beth Morgan (Sian Phillips), anchor of the family,
in an angry confrontation with Elias (Aubrey Richards),
the vengeful, narrow-minded deacon. All the leading
actors were born in Wales. "Death and poverty,"
said actor Baker, of Wales, "were daily threats."

value of the coal was in direct proportion to the danger in mining it, for its combustibility made the coal dust subject to sudden explosions. The coal is also what is called loose-jointed, which makes for loose or rotten roofs. When, just before the First World War, Welsh coal production was at its peak, South Wales also led the world in the number and severity of its accidents, from cave-ins and explosions.

To an innocent student of economics unacquainted with the unchanging status of coal miners through the succeeding ages of feudalism, mercantilism, nineteenth-century capitalism, and twentieth-century industrial democracy, theirs might be assumed to be a privileged and highly paid craft, but for five centuries—from the thirteenth to the end of the eighteenth—they were legally bondsmen bound to the mines for life. When a mine was exhausted or closed down for any other reason, they were compulsorily transferred to other collieries or salt mines. (It is one of the forgotten good deeds of the famous tyrant, George the Third, that in the year of the Declaration of Independence, by an act he forced through Parliament, he broke once for all the coal miner's standing as a bondsman.) But for another hundred years or more, the miners had ten-hour working days, few protections from the perils of the job, and no dependable wages. The notorious "sliding scale" system paid so much a shift, but when production slackened there were fewer shifts and correspondingly lower wages.

In the 1890s, the union movement was just coming to life but then only in the dawning idea that a miner ought to have some say in the terms of his labor. Far off in dreamland in those days were such luxuries as safety laws, ventilation, the pit-head bath, portal-to-portal pay, accident compensation, or any social consideration of "black lung" or of the other health hazards peculiar to miners. It is a hard commentary on what succeeding societies, and opposing ideologies, can come to take for granted that these crippling ailments—and a strong plea for the legal protection of their victims—had been set forth in precise and convincing detail by the Italian epidemiologist, Bernardino Ramazzini, in his pioneer work on occupational disease (*De Morbis Artificum*) published in his eightieth year, in 1713.

After much of a lifetime spent in reporting on all sorts and conditions of labor—from date growers to tattooists, steel workers to ranchers—I can only say that I have nowhere, in America or Britain, felt so much of an uncomfortable and helpless outsider as in the grey, sooty mining villages of West Virginia and South Wales.

225

The story of the abdication of Edward the Eighth is one in which today any competent college history major would expect to get at the least a passing grade. Yet, for great numbers of people—especially Americans—who lived through it, the true reasons why the King had to go are still fudged by what at the time were irrelevancies, though passionately argued, which by now have passed into the popular wisdom. Such as, that the Establishment—the Conservative majority in the House of Commons most of all—balked at the notion of an American-born Queen; that it was alarmed by the King's highly advertised concern ("Something must be done") for the jobless Welsh miners; that the Prime Minister, Mr. Stanley Baldwin, and the Archbishop of Canterbury were shocked by the King's private life (which they were) and on that ground as much as any plotted to force him out (which they didn't); and that the Bishop of Bradford decided to break the dam of official silence by denouncing the King's affair with Mrs. Simpson.

Before we look at the outline of the story, it would be well to say now that the Labor opposition in the House of Commons was, if anything, more adamant than the Conservatives against his staying on the throne; that the prospect of an American consort was never an issue, though that of a twice-divorced one decidedly was; that the King's concern for the condition of the miners was no more than an uncomfortable passing thought; that the Archbishop of Canterbury was consulted only twice, and then rightly as the spiritual head of the state church whose temporal head is the King himself; that the Bishop of Bradford had nothing but this in mind (he had never heard of Mrs. Simpson) when, in a speech protesting a proposal that Nonconformist churchmen be allowed to take part in the Coronation, he casually happened to deplore the King's lax religious habits; and that there is no law or constitutional provision against the King's marrying a commoner or anyone else Parliament approves of—the mother of the present Queen was a commoner, and so is the new Princess of Wales.

When the project of a television drama on Edward the Eighth was mooted, I shared the fears of the people who have seen their worst misgivings realized in the current fashion for docu-dramas: a form that most often threads dazzling little legends on a slender rope of fact in the certainty of manufacturing a "factoid." The more skillfully this is done, the more indelible is the lasting impression. Since it has been proved over and over again, in psychological studies about television, that the thing seen overwhelms in persuasiveness the thing heard, and that the two of them working in unison can disarm rational judgment,

the docu-drama tends to be a narcotic under whose influence the viewer sees a vision, a vivid episode of history fixed once for all—he feels—in essential, if not literal, truth.

Of course, all historical drama is a more or less imaginative re-creation or reassortment of facts and fancies, and no one took more liberties with the genre than Shakespeare. The prejudice of people like me may be that the closer the docu-drama comes to events and personalities of our own time, the more distorted is the evidence on which we may be required to act as citizens (to vote, for instance). The relations of the United States and Iran, I should guess, are likely to be prejudiced for a long time by the TV-implanted memory of the Iranian people as a population of "students" baying day and night outside the American embassy in Teheran for the blood of the hostages.

The first episode of *Edward and Mrs. Simpson* seemed to promise the worst: a picture of the Prince of Wales as the leader of what would now be called the international jet set, disporting itself by day on clothes and gossip and by night on dancing and drinking. But although the triviality of this milieu was not tempered by many reminders of the Prince's court duties—the state papers, the hospital visits, the unceasing round of charity and regimental dinners (at which the Prince was not delinquent)—it turned out to be an astute dramatic device, the setting up of a carefree, cloudless scene on which the impending storm would fall with more thunderous effect.

Four generations: Queen Victoria holds her newborn
great-grandson in 1894, as two kings-to-be—grandfather Edward
VII and father George V—look on. Princeling was
christened Edward Albert Christian George Andrew Patrick
David. He was eldest of George's four sons.

The play moved swiftly thereafter to develop the seriousness of the Prince's new affair, his obsession with it to the exclusion of any constitutional misgivings, and to suggest his ministers' anxiety (once he was King) over his political insensitivity to the rise of Hitler and Mussolini. The last five episodes were, boldly and with much subtle and satisfying detail, about the nub of the affair: the conflict between Parliament's knowledge of the constitutional limits on a king's choice of a wife, and the King's dogged unawareness of them; either of the force of precedent (which had pushed James the Second off the throne) or of any understanding that his fate rested not alone with the judgment of the House of Commons but with the veto power of his "Dominions beyond the seas," namely with the judgment of Canada, Australia, New Zealand, India, and South Africa.

No doubt the most fortunate thing that happened in the planning of this television series was the employment of Frances Donaldson as the script adviser. Her biography (*Edward the Eighth*) is as close to a definitive work as any in our time is likely to be. In no other docu-drama I have seen is there so much authenticated dialogue as that in *Edward and Mrs. Simpson*. All the debates in the House of Commons were taken verbatim from Hansard, the official parliamentary record. There is biographical or documentary evidence for the accuracy of many other scenes: all Baldwin's interviews with the King, with Queen Mary, with the Archbishop; the shuttling consultations between the protagonists and Walter Monckton, the King's lawyer; even, and improbably, for the highly sentimental scene of Winston Churchill's farewell visit to the King.

These rare tokens of authenticity were all the more convincing by the casting of many players who, in looks and bearing, bore an extraordinary resem-

Left: King Edward VIII (Edward Fox) signs the
instrument of abdication by which he will surrender the crown
and marry Wallis Warfield Simpson. Right: Photograph
of Edward, England's first bachelor king in 176 years, as
he broadcast his farewell in March, 1936.

blance to the originals, most notably Nigel Hawthorne as Walter Monckton (who just about stole the series), David Waller as Baldwin, Patrick Troughton as Clement Attlee, Peggy Ashcroft as Queen Mary. Edward Fox's willful weakness was greatly reinforced by the exact timbre and inflections of Edward the Eighth's voice. (I write as one who covered the abdication, in London, for the National Broadcasting Company, night and day during the shattering ten days that followed on the Bishop of Bradford's unwitting thunderbolt.)

In brief, the King wanted to marry Mrs. Simpson and, at first, with his hazy knowledge of the British constitution, he thought it might be contrived through an alliance between certain members of Parliament and a supporting campaign drummed up in the newspapers by press barons. The newspaper proprietors were powerless to do this even if they had been of one mind, which they weren't, but they were able—to the astonishment of the American press corps in London and in long retrospect of the British themselves—to impose an absolute censorship on all printed mention of the affair, until the Bishop of Bradford's innocent gaffe, by which time the King had made up his mind to go.

In the flux of argument and partisanship as it invaded the House of Commons and flooded the newspapers, two insuperable obstacles stood in Edward's way, one intangible, the other a document that can very much be touched and seen.

The intangible was what was long known as "the Nonconformist conscience," the stern, chapel-going respectability of the middle and working classes that had set itself up as a barometer of public behavior with the rise of Gladstone and the Liberal party, and as a guide to political conduct by the succeeding Labor majorities in the House of Commons. Mrs. Simpson's two divorces were wholly unacceptable to all but a fraction of Tory members of Parliament. Neither Edward nor his friends (Mrs. Simpson least of all) had much inkling of the strength of the feeling in the solid parts of the country where it counted. And Winston Churchill's uncharacteristically wild flirtation with the idea of a King's Party doused any flickering hope that Parliament could be ousted as the keeper of the constitution—whose only, but vital, function is to define and protect the power of the people, through Parliament, against the power of the monarchy.

The tangible obstacle was one fairly recent document of the constitution that left the King no choice but to abdicate or give up Mrs. Simpson. In his last outburst of petulance, he had to be instructed about it. It is the Statute of Westminster, passed by Parliament in 1931. And its fatally applicable clause

states: "Any alteration in the law touching the Succession of the Throne or the Royal Style and Titles shall hereafter require the assent as well of the Parliaments of all the Dominions as of the Parliament of the United Kingdom."

If the Nonconformist conscience, and the prejudice it generated against the prospect of a twice-divorced Queen, were still a powerful force in British life in the 1930s, they were more dominant still in the Dominions, colonized mostly by adventurers, entrepreneurs, Methodists, and working-class types to whom middle-class respectability on the Victorian model was to become the cement of their social stability. In the end, the Prime Minister, Mr. Baldwin, dutifully instructed the Secretary of State for the Dominions to offer them a choice of the three proposed possible solutions: a marriage which would establish Mrs. Simpson as the Queen; a morganatic marriage in which she would forfeit the title; or the abdication of the King. India was divided on religious grounds, and New Zealand would agree with whatever Westminster decided. The other three were firm for abdication. So, after all the fratricidal dissensions of the royal family, the press barons, the bishops, the members of Parliament, and other high-placed people in the know, it was the remote citizens of Australia, Canada, and South Africa who brought in the verdict.

On the night after the abdication instrument was signed and read to both Houses of Parliament, Edward—soon to be the Duke of Windsor—sailed from England in a destroyer and left the throne in the keeping of George the Sixth, his wife, Elizabeth, and their two small daughters.

The cast assembles on set. King George and Queen Mary are seated, Edward stands between them. Left of him are Mrs. Simpson and, in minor parts, onetime film stars Jessie Matthews and Bessie Love. Right are Duchess and Duke of York, and Stanley Baldwin.

*Left: Pensive Prince Edward as naval officer
(1907). From the series: The uncrowned King
attends opening of Parliament. Below: Edward
Fox as Edward–or David, as the family
called him–and Cynthia Harris as Mrs. Simpson.
They became Duke and Duchess of Windsor.*

Danger UXB" was a phrase which, after September 1940, Britons in or near London came to know and dread. It was printed or scrawled on signposts or walls wherever there was known, or thought, to be an unexploded German bomb.

In the long and florid history of the movies about the Second World War, which have gone from the evacuation of Dunkirk to the attack on Pearl Harbor, from lonely Yanks in London to Errol Flynn saving Burma single-handed, it is remarkable that no big studio appears to have spotted the dramatic possibilities of a small detachment of the Royal Engineers whose terrifying speciality was that of defusing these delayed-action bombs with which the Germans, during and after the Blitz on Britain, hoped to immobilize much war work and destroy the morale of the people who had survived the night bombings.

It was left to John Hawkesworth, who conceived and produced *Upstairs, Downstairs* and *The Duchess of Duke Street,* to buy up, in the late 1960s, the dramatic rights to the memoir of one Major A. B. Hartley. Once Hawkesworth had exhausted his long preoccupation with the Edwardians, he tapped the memories and the expertise of half-a-dozen surviving officers of the bomb-disposal squads and dramatized Major Hartley's work under its original title, *Danger UXB.* The whole story turned on the experience of a single squad—Section 347 of the Royal Engineers. Applying the same artfulness that he had shown in humanizing the First World War episodes of *Upstairs, Downstairs,* Hawkesworth

Lt. Brian Ash (Anthony Andrews) listens for fateful ticking of an UXB, surrounded by sappers Salt, Mulley, and Powell (Kenneth Cranham, Gordon Kane, and Robert Pugh), and the reliable Sergant James (Maurice Roëves) of Section 347, Royal Engineers.

managed somehow to bring cunning and sentimental changes on what was, after all, the regular anxiety of every one of the twelve episodes: when would the bomb go off?

We have to go back a little into the history of the Blitz, and Hitler's strategical ambitions for it, to see how and why the unexploded bomb was what the Prime Minister, Winston Churchill, called it: "A new and damaging form of attack against us."

The Nazis started the so-called Battle of Britain in the summer of 1940 with sporadic daytime raids on the South Coast, and then on London and the surrounding counties. They were intended to freeze transport, hamper production, and wear down the working population. They didn't work, for two reasons.

The German planes were only eighteen miles from the South Coast, where there was little or no industry, but they were seventy miles or so from London, and in 1940 they didn't have the fuel to do more than bomb a chosen target and wheel for the home run.

Secondly, the British fighter planes appeared to be innumerable and everywhere. There were, in fact, few squadrons. But, after years of research by Germans, British, Italians, and Americans, two British high-frequency experts developed a multicavity magnetron that, just in time for the war, made practical the use of microwave radar. This device helped the fighters to appear to be everywhere at once by enabling them to detect the flight path of incoming raiders, engage them, often to harry and decoy them up-country, until they had no fuel for the return journey. The result was extremely heavy German losses. Hitler saw that he could not invade Britain until he had control of the air over London, and he decided to paralyze the capital city with saturation night bombing. In September 1940, he mounted the Blitz.

In the murky dawn after night raids, people occasionally stumbled on half-buried objects that looked like small, squat torpedoes. It was assumed they were dud bombs. Churchill knew better. He recalled his experience, in the 1914–18 war, of the Germans' use of delayed-action fuses. And he guessed, correctly, that the Germans would improve them. Within a week of the start of the Blitz, he sent off a series of memoranda to the Cabinet ministers responsible for war, for supply, for home security. This is a typical one:

To Secretary of State for War: As I telephoned last night, it is of the highest importance to cope with the UXBs in London, and especially on the railways. The congestion in the marshalling yards is becoming acute.

At his prodding, special units—bomb-disposal squads—were recruited from the Royal Engineers. They consisted of an officer, a sergeant, and six or seven men. Their exclusive job was to render harmless the unexploded bombs. In the beginning, the squads had nothing better to go on than a hammer and chisel, block and tackle, an old manual, and crossed fingers. Their only training came from Royal Air Force officers demonstrating British bomb fuses. Experimental teams wheeled bombs to open ground and, as often as not, were injured or killed in the process. The actual defusing was to be done only by officers, who accordingly were given a transfer option after six months. Surprisingly, few of them took it, although the life expectancy of a new bomb-disposal officer was ten weeks. In the first four months—from September to Christmas 1940—125 bomb-disposal officers lost their lives.

Throughout the winter of 1940–41, the Nazi bombers did immense physical damage to London and drove the Londoners into sleeping quarters in the subways, in cellars and basements, and in rapidly manufactured bomb-resistant (not bomb-proof) shelters. But after three months of night bombing, Hitler had failed to gain control of the air over the city. Bigger bombers and new navigational devices, however, made it possible for him to shift the aerial offensive to the industrial centers of the Midlands and the North. The UXBs were to concentrate on the industrial nerve centers of London. Before the war, German intelligence had constructed—among many accurate maps of London—a series that precisely sited electric grids, power stations, railroad depots, reservoirs, sewage outfalls, and the like. Churchill confessed his fears to his diary:

I was worried principally on two counts. The first was the drains. . . . Could we keep the sewage system working or would there be a pestilence? What would happen if the drains got into the water supply? Early in October, the main London sewage outfall was destroyed, and we had to let all our sewage flow into the Thames, which stank—first of sewage, and afterwards of the floods of chemicals we poured into it. Secondly, I feared that the long nights for millions in the crowded street-shelters (and tube stations) would produce epidemics of influenza, diphtheria, the

*From left: Bomb damage, sapper Salt and mates rig a block
and tackle to free a young woman pinned under a live
bomb, a sapper killed in error, Ash with professor's machine
to steam out explosives, Brian and Susan (Judy Geeson),
whose love counterpoints the violence.*

common cold and what not. But it appeared that Nature had already provided against this danger. Man is a gregarious animal, and apparently the mischievous microbes he exhales fight and neutralize each other. They go out and devour each other, and Man walks off unharmed. If this is not scientifically correct, it ought to be.

The fact was attested later that during the first rough winter the health of the Londoners was above the peacetime average. And, for all the material damage, the loss and mutilation of civilian life, the fearful nighttime racket, and the stupefying lack of sleep, the morale of ordinary people held. "It did not matter where the blow fell," Churchill boasted, "the nation was sound as the sea is salt."

But if life became surprisingly less fearful for the mass of the population, the life of the bomb-disposal squads grew more testy and hazardous as the Nazis improved the bomb types. They had started with a bomb that could be neutralized by unscrewing the locking ring and sliding out the fuse. Very soon they had a bomb on which the act of defusing triggered a spring detonator. This peril was solved by a Cambridge scientist who, noticing that the explosive was soluble, bypassed the fuse by steaming out the explosive. But the Germans always seemed to learn about the British countermoves against their new moves. They developed a bomb expressly designed to dispose of the bomb disposers; the fuse was set to kill anybody who knew the trick of disarming it. Afterward came the "butterfly bombs," tiny bombs that could be sprayed on a village like a cloud of locusts and nestle for days or weeks in bales of hay, tree tops, church steeples, and every other sort of nook and cranny. An alarming dimension was given to this "new and damaging form of attack" with naval mines dropped by parachute. They were of a weight and explosive power and range that made tragic nonsense of Hitler's claim to be aiming only at military targets. (For the first time, the bomb-disposal squads had to defer to the Navy.) In a memo to the military head of the War Cabinet Churchill wrote:

235

At 5,000 feet, he cannot have the slightest idea what he is going to hit. It is an act of terror against the civilian population. I wish to know what is the worst form of equal retaliation we can inflict upon ordinary German cities. . . . Let me have practical proposals by Saturday night.

The practical proposals provoked strong objections, both moral and technical, but in the end the restraints of "strategic bombing" were more or less abandoned by both sides. Coventry was countered by Dresden.

Once Hitler went into Russia, it was generally assumed that he had postponed, at least, all plans for an invasion of Britain. It was not an assumption the British government dared act on. There was an inside rumor of new and more lethal weapons—confirmed in the launching of the German ballistic missiles, V1 and V2, against Britain in the fall of 1944—and Hitler was known to have insisted on the primacy of the war in the West long after the Allied invasion of Europe. But by September 1943, at the latest, the prospect of a German invasion of England was remote. The Nazi armies in North Africa had surrendered to General Omar Bradley. The Allied invasion of Sicily was complete. In Britain, the Nazis—whose air force was mainly engaged on the Russian front—were reduced to infrequent hit-and-run raids and the dropping of more and trickier UXBs. The long tension of the Battle of Britain was broken, a fact officially acknowledged when the railroads were allowed to lift their·ban on the shipping of flowers from Scotland to the South.

The bomb-disposal squads now began their final chore: the very dangerous one of clearing the mines the British themselves had laid down, in 1940, along the piers and coastline of the South and East against the certainty, as it seemed then, of a German invasion. Even after V-E Day, the squads were not entirely disbanded. Long after the war, squad veterans were called on to get to a farm, a railroad yard, a cricket ground, or wherever to defuse a bomb that had lain comatose for as many as ten or twenty years.

Looking back at the work of the bomb-disposal squads when the war was over, Churchill wrote:

Teams were formed which had good or bad luck. Some—a few—survived this phase of our ordeal. Others ran twenty, thirty, or even forty courses before they met their fate. The Unexploded Bomb Detachments presented themselves wherever I went on my tours. Somehow or other, their faces seemed different from those of ordinary men, however brave or faithful. They were gaunt, they were haggard, their faces had a bluish look, with bright gleaming eyes and exceptional compression of the lips; withal a perfect demeanour. In writing about our hard times, we are apt to over-use the word grim. It should have been reserved for the UXB Disposal Squads.

Masterpiece Theatre Chronology

THE FIRST CHURCHILLS
January 10–March 28, 1971
Produced by: BBC
Original story by Donald Wilson
Dramatized by Donald Wilson
Producer: Donald Wilson
Director: David Giles
Cast:
  Susan Hampshire   Sheila Gish
  John Neville   John Saunders
  John Standing   Margaret Tyzack
  James Villiers
  John Westbrook

THE SPOILS OF POYNTON
April 4–April 25, 1971
Produced by: BBC
Based on the novel by Henry James
Dramatized by Lennox Phillips
Producer: Martin Lisemore
Director: Peter Sasdy
Cast
  June Ellis
  Diane Fletcher
  Pauline Jameson
  Gemma Jones
  Ian Oglivy

THE POSSESSED
May 2–June 6, 1971
Produced by: BBC
Based on the novel by: Feodor Dostoyevsky
Dramatized by: Lennox Phillips
Producer: David Conroy
Director: Naomi Capon
Cast:
  Keith Bell   Joseph O'Connor
  Eve Belton   Tim Preece
  David Collings   Anne Stallybrass
  Rosalie Crutchley

PERE GORIOT
June 13–July 4, 1971
Produced by: BBC
Based on the novel by Honoré de Balzac
Dramatized by David Turner
Producer: David Conroy
Director: Paddy Russel
Cast:
  Angela Browne   Walter Gotell
  Anna Cropper   Andrew Keir
  David Dundas   Moira Redmond
  Michael Goodliffe June Ritchie

JUDE THE OBSCURE
October 3–November 7, 1971
Produced by: BBC
Based on the novel by Thomas Hardy
Dramatized by Harry Green
Producer: Martin Lisemore
Director: Hugh David
Cast:
  Daphne Heard
  Alex Marshall
  Robert Powell
  John Franklyn Robbins
  Fiona Walker

THE GAMBLER
November 14–November 21, 1971
Produced by: BBC
Based on the novel by Feodor Dostoyevsky
Dramatized by John Hopkins
Producer: David Conroy
Director: Michael Ferguson
Cast:
  Dame Edith Evans   Colin Redgrave
  Philip Madoc   Maurice Roëves
  John Phillips   Georgina Ward

RESURRECTION
November 28–December 19, 1971
Produced by: BBC
Based on the novel by Leo Tolstoy
Dramatized by Alexander Baron
Producer: David Conroy
Cast:
  John Bryans   Brian Murphy
  Alan Dobie   Pam Ruddock
  Athene Fielding   Bridget Turner
  Tina Mathews   Mitzi Webster

COLD COMFORT FARM
December 6, 1971
Produced by: BBC
Based on the novel by Stella Gibbons
Dramatized by David Turner
Producer: David Conroy
Director: Peter Hammond
Cast:
  Sarah Badel   Rosalie Crutchley
  Joan Bakewell   Peter Egan
  Brian Blessed   Alastair Sim
  Fay Compton   Freddie Jones

THE SIX WIVES OF HENRY THE EIGHTH
January 1–February 6, 1972
Produced by: BBC
Based on an idea by Maurice Cowan
Original dramas by:
  Beverley Cross   John Prebble
  Nick McCarty   Rosemary Anne Sisson
  Jean Morris   Ian Thorne
Producers: Mark Shivas, Ronald Travers
Directors: Naomi Capon, John Glenister
Cast:
  Annette Crosbie   Angela Pleasence
  Rosalie Crutchley Anne Stallybrass
  Elvi Hale   Patrick Troughton
  Keith Michell   Dorothy Tutin

ELIZABETH R
February 13–March 19, 1972
Produced by: BBC
Producer: Roderick Graham
Original dramas by:
  John Hale   Ian Rodger
  Julian Mitchell   Rosemary Sisson
  John Prebble   Hugh Whitemore
Directors:
  Roderick Graham   Claude Whatham
  Richard Martin   Herbert Wise
  Donald McWhinnie
Cast:
  Rosalie Crutchley Glenda Jackson
  Robin Ellis   Peter Jeffrey
  Sarah Frampton   Jason Kemp
  Robert Hardy   Stephen Murray
  Ronald Hines   Vivian Pickles

THE LAST OF THE MOHICANS
March 26–May 14, 1972
Produced by: BBC
Based on the novel by James Fenimore Cooper
Dramatized by Harry Green
Producer: John McRae
Director: David Maloney
Cast:
  John Abineri   Philip Madoc
  Andrew Crawford   Patricia Maynard
  Tim Goodman   Richard Warwick
  Kenneth Ives   Joanna David

VANITY FAIR
October 1–October 29, 1972
Produced by: BBC
Based on the novel
  by William Makepeace Thackeray
Dramatized by Rex Tucker
Producer: David Conroy
Director: David Giles
Cast:
  Richard Caldicot   Bryan Marshall
  Susan Hampshire   John Moffatt
  Dyson Lovell   Marilyn Taylerson
  Roy Marsden

COUSIN BETTE
November 5–December 3, 1972
Produced by: BBC
Based on the novel by Honoré Balzac
Dramatized by Ray Lawler
Producer: Martin Lisemore
Director: Gareth Davies
Cast:
  John Bryans
  Esmond Knight
  Ursula Howells
  Helen Mirren
  Margaret Tyzack
  Thorley Walters

THE MOONSTONE
December 10, 1972–January 7, 1973
Produced by: BBC
Based on the novel by Wilkie Collins
Dramatized by Hugh Leonard
Cast:
  Colin Baker   Robin Ellis
  Derek Chafer   Vivien Heilbron
  Anna Cropper   Martin Jarvis
  Basil Dignam   John Welsh

TOM BROWN'S SCHOOLDAYS
January 14–February 11, 1973
Produced by: BBC
Based on the novel by Thomas Hughes
Dramatized by Anthony Stevens
Producer: John McRae
Director: Gareth Davies
Cast:
  Iain Cuthbertson   Anthony Murphy
  Gerald Flood   John Paul
  Richard Morant   Simon Turner

POINT COUNTERPOINT
February 18–March 18, 1973
Produced by: BBC
Based on the novel by Aldous Huxley
Dramatized by Simon Raven
Producer: David Conroy
Director: Rex Tucker
Cast:

Max Adrian	Valerie Gearon
Lyndon Brook	Patricia English
David Collings	Sheila Grant
Noel Dyson	Tristram Jellinek

THE GOLDEN BOWL
March 25–April 29, 1973
Produced by: BBC
Based on the novel by Henry James
Dramatized by Jack Pulman
Producer: Martin Lisemore
Director: James Cellan Jones
Cast:

Kathleen Byron	Daniel Massey
Cyril Cusack	Barry Morse
Gayle Hunnicutt	Jill Townsend

CLOUDS OF WITNESS
October 7–November 4, 1973
Produced by: BBC
Based on the novel by Dorothy Sayers
Dramatized by Anthony Steven
Producer: Richard Beynon
Director: Hugh David
Cast:

Anthony Ainley	Rachel Herbert
Ian Carmichael	Charles Hodgson
Noel Coleman	Glyn Houston
Mark Eden	David Langton
Petronella Ford	

THE MAN WHO WAS HUNTING HIMSELF
November 11–November 25, 1973
Produced by: BBC
Original drama by N. J. Crisp
Producer: Bill Sellers
Director: Terence Williams
Cast:

Carol Austin	Robin Hawdon
Lois Baxter	Garfield Morgan
Donald Burton	David Savile

THE UNPLEASANTNESS AT THE
    BELLONA CLUB
December 2–December 23, 1973
Produced by: BBC
Based on the novel by Dorothy L. Sayers
Dramatized by John Bowen
Producer: Richard Beynon
Director: Ronald Wilson
Cast:

Terence Alexander	Mark Eden
Ian Carmichael	Phyllida Law
Anna Cropper	John Welsh

THE LITTLE FARM
December 30, 1973
Produced by: Granada International Television
Based on the story by H. E. Bates
Dramatized by Hugh Leonard
Producer: Derek Granger
Director: Silvio Narizzano
Cast:

Michael Elphick
Barbara Ewing
Diane Keen
Bryan Marshall

UPSTAIRS, DOWNSTAIRS (I)
January 6–March 31, 1974
Produced by: London Weekend Television
Producer: John Hawkesworth
Original dramas by:

Terence Brady	Alfred Shaughnessy
Charlotte Bingham	Rosemary Anne Sisson
John Hawkesworth	Anthony Skene
Jeremy Paul	Fay Weldon

Directors:

Bill Bain	Raymond Menmuir
Cyril Coke	Herbesrt Wise
Chris Hodson	

Cast:

John Alderton	David Langton
Angela Baddeley	Jean Marsh
Christopher Beeny	Meg Wynn Owen
Pauline Collins	Nicola Pagett
Rachel Gurney	Patsy Smart
George Innes	Jenny Thomasin
Gordon Jackson	Simon Williams

THE EDWARDIANS
July 7–July 28, 1974
Produced by: BBC
Producer: Mark Shivas

"Lloyd George"
Dramatized by Keith Dewhurst
Director: John Davies
Cast:

Annette Crosbie
Anthony Hopkins
Thorley Walters

"The Reluctant Juggler"
Dramatized by Alan Plater
Director: John Davies
Cast:

Georgia Brown
Jack Douglas
Fulton MacKay
Peter Pratt
George Sewell

"Mr. Rolls and Mr. Royce"
Dramatized by Ian Curteis
Director: Gerald Blake
Cast:

Michael Jayston
Robert Powell

"Conan Doyle"
Dramatized by Jeremy Paul
Director: Brian Farnham
Cast:

Maria Aitken
Nigel Davenport
Alison Leggatt
Preston Lockwood

MURDER MUST ADVERTISE
October 6–October 28, 1974
Produced by: BBC
Based on the novel by Dorothy L. Sayers
Dramatized by Bill Craig
Producer: Richard Beynon
Director: Rodney Bennett
Cast:

Bridget Armstrong	Dian de Momerie
Robin Bailey	Mark Eden
Peter Bowles	Rachel Herbert
Ian Carmichael	Fiona Walker
Paul Darrow	

UPSTAIRS, DOWNSTAIRS (II)
November 3, 1974–January 26, 1975
Produced by: London Weekend Television
Producer: John Hawkesworth
Original dramas by:

John Hawkesworth	Alfred Shaughnessy
Deborah Mortimer	Rosemary Anne Sisson
Jeremy Paul	Anthony Skene

Directors:

Bill Bain	Lionel Harris
Derek Bennett	Chris Hodson
Cyril Coke	

COUNTRY MATTERS (I)
February 2–February 23, 1975
Produced by: Granada International Television
Series devised by Derek Granger
Producer: Derek Granger
Based on stories by A. E. Coppard and
    H. E. Bates
Dramatizations by Hugh Leonard and
    James Saunders
Directors:

Barry Davis	Richard Martin
John Mackenzie	Donald McWhinnie

Cast:

Rosalind Ayres	Glyn Houston
Maria Charles	Robert Keegan
Stephen Chase	Jane Lapotaire
Rosalie Crutchley	Gareth Thomas
Keith Drinkel	John Welsh
Susan Fleetwood	Mary Wimbush

VIENNA 1900
March 2–April 6, 1981
Produced by: BBC
Based on the stories by Arthur Schnitzler
Dramatized by Roger Muller
Producer: Richard Beynon
Director: Herbert Wise
Cast:

Christopher Gable	Lynn Redgrave
Christopher Guard	Robert Stephens
Venessa Miles	Fiona Walker
Maureen O'Brien	Dorothy Tutin

THE NINE TAILORS
April 13–May 4, 1975
Produced by: BBC
Based on the novel by Dorothy L. Sayers
Dramatized by Anthony Stevens
Producer: Richard Beynon
Director: Raymond Menmuir
Cast:

Elizabeth Bradley	Keith Drinkel
Edwin Brown	Donald Eccles
Ian Carmichael	Glyn Houston

SHOULDER TO SHOULDER
October 5–November 9, 1975
Produced by: BBC in association with
    Warner Bros. Television, Ltd.
Producer: Verity Lambert
Original dramas by:

Douglas Livingstone	Ken Taylor
Alan Plater	Hugh Whitemore

Directors: Moira Armstrong and Waris Hussein
Cast:

Sheila Allen	Fulton Mackay
Georgia Brown	Johnathan Newth
Patience Collier	Judy Parfitt
Angela Down	Sian Phillips
Michael Gough	Maureen Pryor
Robert Hardy	Patricia Quinn
Ronald Hines	

NOTORIOUS WOMAN
November 16–December 28, 1975
Produced by: BBC in association with
　Warner Bros. Television, Ltd.
Original drama by Harry W. Junkin
Producer: Pieter Rogers
Director: Waris Hussein
Cast:

George Chakiris	Jeremy Irons
Shenead Cusack	Cathleen Nesbit
Lewis Fiander	Johnathan Newth
Rosemary Harris	Joyce Redman
Alan Howard	Leon Vitali

UPSTAIRS, DOWNSTAIRS (III)
January 4–March 28, 1976
Produced by: London Weekend Television
Producer: John Hawkesworth
Original dramas by:
　John Hawkesworth
　Elizabeth Jane Howard
　Jeremy Paul
　Alfred Shaughnessy
　Rosemary Anne Sisson
Directors:

Bill Bain	Lionel Harris
Derek Bennett	Christopher Hodson
Cyril Coke	

CAKES AND ALE
April 4–April 18, 1976
Produced by: BBC
Based on the novel by Somerset Maugham
Dramatized by Harry Green
Producer: Harry Green
Director: Bill Hays
Cast:

Judy Cornwell	Michael Hordern
Lynn Farleigh	Peter Jeffrey
James Grout	Mike Pratt

SUNSET SONG
April 25–May 30, 1976
Produced by: BBC
Based on the novel by Lewis Grassic Gibbon
Dramatized by Bill Craig
Producer: Pharic Maclaren
Director: Moira Armstrong
Cast:
　Derek Anders
　Victor Carin
　James Grant
　John Grieve
　Vivien Heilbron
　Andrew Keir
　Anne Kristen
　Edith Macarthur
　Roddy McMillan
　Paul Young

MADAME BOVARY
October 10–October 31, 1976
Based on the novel by Gustave Flaubert
Dramatized by Giles Cooper
Producer: Richard Beynon
Director: Rodney Bennett
Cast:

Francesca Annis	Ray Smith
Tom Conti	Brian Stirner
Denis Lill	

HOW GREEN WAS MY VALLEY
November 7–December 12, 1976
Produced by: BBC and 20th Century Fox
　Television
Based on the novel by Richard Llewellyn
Producer: Martin Lisemore
Director: Ronald Wilson
Cast:

Stanley Baker	Victoria Plucknett
Keith Drinkel	Aubrey Richards
Mike Gwilyn	Clive Roberts
Sian Phillips	Justin Smith
Rhys Powys	Gareth Thomas

FIVE RED HERRINGS
December 19, 1976–January 9, 1977
Produced by: BBC
Based on the novel by Dorothy L. Sayers
Dramatized by Anthony Steven
Producer: Bill Sellars
Director: Robert Tronson
Cast:

Ian Carmichael	John Junkin
Glyn Houston	David McKail
Russell Hunter	David Rintoul
Ian Ireland	

UPSTAIRS, DOWNSTAIRS (IV)
January 16–May 1, 1977
Produced by: London Weekend Television
Producer: John Hawkesworth
Original dramas by:

John Hawkesworth	Alfred Shaughnessy
Jeremy Paul	Rosemary Anne Sisson

Directors:

Bill Bain	Christopher Hodson
Derek Bennett	Simon Langton
Cyril Coke	James Ormerod

Additional Cast:

Joan Benham	Hannah Gordon
Lesley-Anne Down	Raymond Huntley
Karen Dotrice	Gordon Jackson

POLDARK (I)
　May 8–August 21, 1977
Produced by: BBC in association with
　London Film Productions, Ltd.
Producer: Morris Barry
Based on the novels by Winston Graham
Dramatizations by:

Peter Draper	Jack Russell
Jack Pulman	Paul Wheeler

Directors:
　Paul Annett
　Christopher Barry
　Kenneth Ives
Cast:

John Baskcomb	Judy Geeson
Ralph Bates	Richard Morant
Paul Curran	Angharad Rees
Donald Douglas	Jill Townsend
Robin Ellis	Tilly Tremayne
Clive Francis	Mary Wimbush

DICKENS OF LONDON
August 28–October 30, 1977
Produced by: Yorkshire Television
Original television series written by
Wolf Mankowitz
Producer: Marc Miller
Directors: Marc Miller and Michael Ferguson
Cast:

Simon Bell	Gene Foad
Diana Coupland	Raymond Francis
Roy Dotrice	Holly Palance

I, CLAUDIUS
November 6, 1977–January 30, 1978
Produced by: BBC, in association with
　London Film Productions, Ltd.
Based on the novels by Robert Graves
Dramatized by Jack Pulman
Producer: Martin Lisemore
Director: Herbert Wise
Cast:

George Baker	Ian Ogilvy
Brian Blessed	John Paul
Lyndon Brook	Sian Phillips
David Davenport	Patricia Quinn
Freda Dowie	Aubrey Richards
James Faulkener	David Robb
Christopher Guard	Patrick Stewart
Richard Hunter	Fiona Walker
John Hurt	Frances White
Derek Jacobi	Sheila White
Beth Morris	

ANNA KARENINA
February 5–April 9, 1978
Produced by: BBC
Based on the novel by Leo Tolstoy
Dramatized by Donald Wilson
Producer: Donald Wilson
Director: Basil Coleman
Cast:

David Harries	Nicola Pagett
Caroline Langrishe	Eric Porter
Mary Morris	Robert Swann
Carol Nimmons	Stuart Wilson

OUR MUTUAL FRIEND
April 16–May 28, 1978
Produced by: BBC
Based on the novel by Charles Dickens
Dramatized by Julia Jones and
　Donald Churchill
Producer: Martin Lisemore
Director: Peter Hammond
Cast:

Lesley Dunlop	John McEnery
Kathleen Harrison	Leo McKern
Polly James	Jane Seymour
Nicholas Jones	Jack Wild

POLDARK (II)
June 4–August 27, 1978
Produced by: BBC, in association with
　London Film Productions, Ltd.
Based on the novels by Winston Graham
Dramatized by:
　Alexander Baron
　John Wiles
　Martin Worth
Producers: Tony Coburn and
　Richard Beynon
Directors: Philip Dudley and Roger Jenkins

THE MAYOR OF CASTERBRIDGE
September 3–October 15, 1978
Produced by: BBC
Based on the novel by Thomas Hardy
Dramatized by Dennis Potter
Producer: Jonathan Powell
Director: David Giles
Cast:

Alan Bates	Anna Massey
Avis Brunage	Janet Maw
Anthony Douse	Ann Stallybrass
Jack Galloway	

THE DUCHESS OF DUKE STREET (I)
October 22, 1978–January 28, 1979
Produced by: BBC-TV/Time-Life Television
  Co-Production
Producer: John Hawkesworth
Original dramas by:
  Julian Bond   Julia Jones
  David Butler   Jeremy Paul
  Bill Craig   Jack Rosenthal
  John Hawkesworth   Rosemary Anne Sisson
Directors:
  Bill Bain   Simon Langton
  Cyril Coke   Raymond Menmuir
Cast:
  June Brown   Victoria Plucknett
  John Cater   John Rapley
  Christopher   Richard Vernon
    Cazanove   Lalla Ward
  Holly DeJong   John Welsh
  Mary Healey   Sammie Winmill
  Gemma Jones

COUNTRY MATTERS (II)
February 4–March 4, 1979
Produced by: Granada International Television
Producer: Derek Granger
Based on stories by A. E. Coppard
  and H. E. Bates
Adapted by:
Hugh Leonard
Jeremy Paul
Hugh Whitemore
Directors:
  Barry Davis   Silvio Narizzano
  Richard Everitt   Peter Wood
Cast:
  Rene Asherson   Maggie Fitzgibbon
  Joss Ackland   Morag Hood
  Jeremy Brett   Rachel Kempson
  Pauline Collins   Meg Wynn Owen
  Caroline Courage   Clare Sutcliffe
  Anna Cropper   Robert Urquhart
  Peter Firth   Penelope Wilton

LILLIE
March 11–June 3, 1979
Produced by: London Weekend Television
Producer: Jack Williams
Original dramas by David Butler and
  John Gorrie
Directors:
  John Gorrie
  Christopher Hodson
  Tony Wharmby
Cast:
  Francesca Annis   Patrick Holt
  Cheryl Campbell   Nicholas Joans
  John Castle   Denis Lill
  Joanna David   Jennie Linden
  Peter Egan   Anton Rodgers
  Catherine Feller   James Warwick
  Ann Firbank   Peggy Ann Wood

KEAN
September 9 and 16, 1979
Produced by: BBC
Based on the play by Jean-Paul Sartre
Translated by: Frank Hauser
Producer: David Jones
Director: James Cellan Jones
Cast:
  Adrienne Corri   Cheri Lunghi
  Anthony Hopkins   Frank Middlemass
  Barrie Ingham   Robert Stephens
  Sara Kestleman

LOVE FOR LYDIA
September 23–December 9, 1979
Produced by: London Weekend Television
Based on a novel by H. E. Bates
Dramatized by Julian Bond
Producer: Tony Wharmby
Directors:
  John Glenister   Christopher Hodson
  Piers Haggard   Simon Langton
                         Michael Simpson
                         Tony Wharmby
Cast:
  Michael Aldridge   Jeremy Irons
  Ralph Arliss   Rachel Kempson
  Christopher Blake   Beatrix Lehmann
  Peter Davison   Mel Martin

THE DUCHESS OF DUKE STREET (II)
December 16, 1979–April 6, 1980
Produced by: BBC-TV/Time-Life Television
  Co-Production
Producer: John Hawkesworth
Original dramas by:
  Bill Craig   Jeremy Paul
  John Hawkesworth   Rosemary Sisson
  Julia Jones   Maggie Wadey
Directors:
  Bill Bain   Simon Langton
  Cyril Coke   Gerry Mill

MY SON, MY SON
April 13–May 25, 1980
Produced by: BBC-TV/Time-Life Television
  Co-Production
Based on the novel by Howard Spring
Dramatized by Julian Bond
Producer: Keith Williams
Director: Peter Cregeen
Cast:
  Kate Binchy   Sherrie Hewson
  Patsy Byrne   Ciaran Madden
  Prue Clarke   Allan McClelland
  Julian Fellowes   Patrick Ryecart
  Frank Grimes   Michael Williams

DISRAELI
June 1–June 22, 1980
Produced by: ATV Network Production
Original drama by David Butler
Producer: Cecil Clarke
Director: Claude Whatham
Cast:
  John Carlisle   Aubrey Morris
  Mark Dignam   Mary Peach
  Rosemary Leach   Anton Rodgers
  Jenny Litman   William Russell
  Ian McShane

CRIME AND PUNISHMENT
September 28–October 19, 1980
Produced by: BBC
Based on the novel by Feodor Dostoyevsky
Dramatized by Jack Pulman
Producer: Jonathan Powell
Director: Michael Darlow
Cast:
  Anthony Bate   Yolande Palfrey
  John Hurt   Sian Phillips
  Beatrix Lehman   Carinthia West
  Frank Middlemass   Timothy West

PRIDE AND PREJUDICE
October 26–November 23, 1980
Produced by: BBC
Based on the novel by Jane Austen
Dramatized by Fay Weldon
Producer: Jonathan Powell
Director: Cyril Coke
Cast:
  Osmund Bullock   Natalie Ogle
  Marsha Fitzalan   Tessa Peake-Jones
  Sabina Franklyn   Pete Settelen
  Elizabeth Garvie   Malcolm Rennie
  Claire Higgins   David Rintoul
  Priscilla Morgan   Moray Watson

TESTAMENT OF YOUTH
November 30–December 28, 1980
Produced by: BBC in Association with London
  Film Productions Ltd.
Based on the autobiography by Vera Brittain
Dramatized by Elaine Morgan
Producer: Jonathan Powell
Director: Moira Armstrong
Cast:
  Geoffrey Burridge   Joanna McCallum
  Cheryl Campbell   Francis Tomelty
  Rosalie Crutchley   Michael Troughton
  Hazel Douglas   Jane Wenham
  Rupert Frazer   Peter Woodward
  Emrys James

DANGER UXB
January 4–April 5, 1981
Produced by: Thames Television
Based on the book by Major Bill Hartley
Producer: John Hawkesworth
Directors:
  Roy Ward Baker   Henry Herbert
  Douglan Camfield   Simon Langton
  Ferdinand Fairfax   Jeremy Summers
Cast:
  Anthony Andrews   Gordon Kane
  Norman Chappell   Ken Kitson
  Kenneth Cranham   Robert Longden
  Iain Cuthbertson   Robert Pugh
  Kenneth Farrington   Maurice Roëves
  Judy Geeson   Jeremy Sinden
  George Innes   Deborah Watling

THERESE RAQUIN
April 12–April 26, 1981
Produced by: BBC and London Film
  Productions Co-production
Based on the novel by Emile Zola
Dramatized by Philip Mackie
Producer: Jonathan Powell
Director: Simon Langton
Cast:
  Timothy Bateson   Jenny Galloway
  Philip Bowen   Kate Nelligan
  Brian Cox   Richard Pearson
  Kenneth Cranham   Mona Washbourne

EDWARD & MRS. SIMPSON
starts November 15, 1981
Produced by: Thames Television
Based on the biography by Frances Donaldson
Dramatized by Simon Raven
Producer: Andrew Brown
Director: Waris Hussein
Cast:
  Peggy Ashcroft   Cynthia Harris
  Trevor Bowen   Nigel Hawthorne
  Edward Fox   Wensley Pithey
  Marius Goring   David Waller